The Spiritual Warfare Victory Manual for Christians

Dispel Demonic Interference with the Discernment of Spirits, God's Word, Scriptures, and Spiritual Warfare Prayers for Protection and Deliverance

Caleb E Benedict

Table of Contents

Part 3: Practical Steps Toward Victory on the Battlefront

Introduction

Civilizations from Babylon to contemporary America have faced struggles with the demonic. In Judaic tradition, the Talmud, Midrash, and Mishnah all relate tales of prophets confronting heinous forces through a combination of holy words and force of will. In the New Testament, Jesus demonstrates his most visible divine gifts when casting out demons upon the shores of Galilee and driving out devils from the possessed. In pagan texts from Norse and Celtic traditions, demons often assume more elusive forms, shifting shapes to deceive their human victims. Regardless of which cultural background these accounts belong to, these accounts' cultural backgrounds, commonalities appear again and again. Victims of demonic influence exhibit mental, spiritual, and physical manifestations of the evil presence attempting to hijack their personhood. In the process, they are both themselves and the Other.

In more recent ages, the boundaries between demonic

interference and mental illness have become more prominent since the rise of modern psychological science. In the Middle Ages, cases of demonic possession led to systems of isolation and alienation, such as the Ship of Fools, where those considered "possessed" were quite literally boarded onto ships and set asea. As the Enlightenment clarified our understanding of psychology—and especially with the rise of clinical psychiatry after Wilhelm Wundt, William James, and Sigmund Freud—the role of mental illness in previously diagnosed cases of possession displaced many pre-existing assumptions about the interconnectedness of mind, body, and spirit. At the same time, modern behavioral science has failed to completely dispel cases of demonic possession and interference as mere symptoms of mental dysfunction. Instead, to truly comprehend the scope of demonic interference in the physical realms, we need to grasp these fundamental differences—and in doing so, equip ourselves more completely against any form of negative interference, whether cognitive or spiritual.

Spiritual warfare is the art of combating evil in its various forms. As St. John Chrystostom once stated, "Only those who do not fight are never wounded." This book aims to present you with the tools to identify demonic phenomena, determine whether their source is spiritual or mental, and equip you with strategies to rid yourself or others of these afflictions. Being informed about demons and their dangers is the first step. After all, knowledge is power—but without practical knowledge, anyone wrestling with demonic forces remains powerless against these trespasses against their free will. The techniques in this book involve expanding knowledge of prayers for both defensive and proactive protection. This dual approach allows the [supplicant] to prevent future demonic interference and actively confront and eradicate any currently disrupting their lives. In the process, the afflicted will once again be able to exist as a free human spirit, allowing them to rebuild their lives and pursue a healthy, happy future.

Many people dismiss possession as folklore, superstition, or hoax—until they witness it. Growing up in rural Iowa, I witnessed a local priest perform an exorcism on a woman in the neighborhood who had gone from being a lovely neighbor to an uncontrollable force of destruction. At first, people in town assumed she was facing a mental illness, but the physicians and psychiatrists that saw her could not reach a diagnosis. She had never before exhibited symptoms of any mental disorder, let alone a condition where something seemed to be speaking through her in a language none of them could interpret. The family was noticeably distraught, especially since bizarre occurrences around the house seemed connected to their relative's distress. Only when they sought the assistance of the Diocese did they find any relief. The Monseigneur was an experienced exorcist, and after several sessions with the woman, he managed to cure her and bless her to prevent any future demonic attacks.

Of course, even though the most popular accounts of the

demonic involve Catholic rituals, these confrontations are not limited to the Church alone. In my studies as an anthropologist, I have seen a variety of approaches based on the same principles presented in this book. In a remote South American village, I witnessed a holy man dispel a demonic presence from a young boy who went on to lead an otherwise normal life. As I traveled country to country, from Europe to Southeast Asia to the Pacific Islands, I heard more and more stories that reinforced my belief that these demonic presences were all too real, and that the techniques used to expel them shared the same fundamental principles.

As I began to practice these techniques myself, I also came to understand that no practitioner is perfect and that only through our mistakes can we begin to hone our skills in confronting the demonic. A combination of theory and practice is necessary for any spiritual endeavor, but in spiritual warfare, this combination is even more vital for success in battle. When confronted by a diabolical force, merely understanding the principles behind protection is not enough to achieve victory. By practicing the prayers in our arsenal and living a life in line with the teachings of Christ, we arm ourselves for victory in any situation.

This guide will give you a supreme advantage as you begin your studies in spiritual warfare. Not only will you be able to identify curses and other spells directed against you, but you will now have a spiritual toolkit to solve them and protect yourself from future harm. Beyond just the methods, you will also learn when and why certain prayers are most appropriate and ways to raise your awareness about potential threats to yourself and others. Equipped with this knowledge, you will find that your life circumstances, or those facing demonic challenges, will greatly improve, allowing you to live again in the light without the fear that the spiritual shadow too often brings into our lives.

Everyone has darkness in their life that needs to be dispelled; distinguishing between those that require spiritual warfare and those that require lifestyle changes is also a crucial part of this book. While the temptation to blame our problems on the supernatural can be tempting, we must also realize that each one of us contains the power of positive change within ourselves.

As I mentioned, I have personally encountered demonic forces and seen experts cope with them. But I have also heard stories from around the world making similar claims. According to renowned exorcist Gabriele Amorth, the occurrence of demonic influence in its various forms remains a major source of trouble throughout the world. Similarly, accounts by saints such as Ignatius of Loyola, Catherine of Siena, and Padre Pio testify to the constant threat of demonic interference in our daily lives—and demonstrate how knowledge of the divine can help repel these forces. Accounts by Rabbi Ansky about possession by *dybbuk* or tales of *asuras* by Hindu brahmins further suggest that demons exist among us in many forms. Countless other examples exist, providing further proof that demonic threats exist in all walks of life around the globe—and thankfully, so do the spiritual tools to face them.

This book's pledge to its readers is one rooted in love. After reading this book, you will be equipped with the basic knowledge and practices of spiritual warfare that will allow you to protect yourself and others from evil interferences. You will be able to identify the signs of demonic activity and determine the best tactics for confronting them. You will know how to destroy what needs to be destroyed and protect what needs to be protected. You will learn prayers from one of the most ancient spiritual traditions in the world, ones that provide both protection and serve as weapons against the demonic. Most importantly, you will be empowered with skills that allow you to confront powerful evil while keeping yourself safe as you do so.

Demons present a serious, imminent threat to our world. Possessions, oppressions, negative curses: all these need to be thoroughly understood to dispel them properly. In certain cases, spiritual negativity can stem from previous generations or be more immediate. Many manuals will simply provide a list of prayers without providing the context of when and where to use them. Remember, words alone are usually insufficient when confronting a demonic threat, and this book incorporates a variety of traditions to equip the reader with the most comprehensive spiritual weapons and shields available for beginners. In addition, through these practices, you will better understand yourself, the world, and your place in it.

This book comes from a place of light and love, and therefore serves as a source of that same benevolent power. Demons and the evil they conjure cannot withstand these mighty forces of good if wielded by a practitioner who embraces them completely. Chapter by chapter, you will learn about traditions and techniques, ways to distinguish between the demonic and other negative forces, and how to achieve victory and preserve it. Through accounts of exorcisms, words and deeds of the saints, and practical knowledge of rituals and sacred objects, you will equip yourself for any current battles—and battles yet to come. Most importantly, equipped with the strategies used in the war between Heaven and Hell, you will better understand your own place in the armies of God.

PART 1

Manual of Possession

Good, Evil, and the Modern Mind

The nature of good and evil has occupied thinkers from all schools of thought across cultures and chronologies. Although often seen as opposites in traditions such as Manichaeism, Judaism, and Christianity, the Modern Mind has come to understand good and evil in slightly different terms. Friedrich Nietzsche famously asserted that the modern mind is beyond good and evil. In his influential work Beyond Good and Evil, Nietzsche claims that philosophy and religion have too long thought in absolutes when it comes to good and evil and that morality forces all actions into a misleading set of opposites based on outdated ethical codes. Despite these arguments, the question of evil remains one worth asking. After all, any perceptive person can trace sources of evil in the world, whether war between nations or war within ourselves. Yet before we can trace these sources, we must first ask a fundamental question about evil itself. What is evil? Perhaps one of the most convincing definitions comes from noted scholar Henry van Dyke, who claimed that to understand evil, we must accept three principles. First, evil is "that which ought not to be." Second, we must admit that evil actually exists in the world. Third, evil "is contrary to that which ought to be." In other words, evil exists as a contradiction to the divine plan of reality, a kind of cosmic cancer.

Evil surrounds us; this much is clear. Whether in negative energy, tragic life events, or a disturbing presence, evil constantly threatens our spiritual well-being. But what can we do about it? More urgently, how can we know what type of evil we are confronting? In war, the sides are not always clearly delineated, and in wars of the spirit, they are even more difficult to discern. In our modern era of skepticism, we can easily blame evil actions on social problems, mental diseases, or political boogeymen. But when we encounter evil in our lives— undeniable spiritual evil which defies rational explanation—we must not only equip ourselves with weapons to combat it but also fortify ourselves with the proper shields against its influence. The first step in arming ourselves is knowing when we are in the presence of such evil.

Are you under an attack? Signs of Possession

Those who have been in the presence of genuine evil

understand on a visceral level what such a force feels like: we experience nausea, anxiety, and otherworldly agitation. But how can we be certain that we are facing a supernatural threat? One of the most important skills for beginners is determining whether you are under attack by a demonic force. Determining the signs of possession poses several problems for the uninitiated. First, possession must be distinguished from other forms of demonic interference, such as vexation, obsession, and infestation (which will be discussed in Part 2). Unlike these other forms of diabolical influence, possession involves the complete occupation of the body by a profane otherworldly force.

The first sign of possession is a drastic personality change. This change is more than simply a mood swing or emotional breakdown but a complete shift in attitude and behavior. Oftentimes, the possessed person later admits that they have little or no memory of the possession itself, so complete is the takeover of their bodies. As T. K. Osterreich notes in Possession, Demoniacal and Other (1963), classic possession cases follow a similar pattern. These early behavioral changes are followed by restlessness and outbursts, followed by violence. This physical embodiment of Wrath leads to "fits," where the afflicted flails and curses uncontrollably. William Sargant notes in The Mind Possessed that these fits are not the same as epileptic seizures, although they share many similarities. Epileptic fits are treatable by medical means such as sedatives, whereas possession resists any medical intervention. In extreme cases, other supernatural events occur, such as objects moving around the room, mysterious voices, and strange odors.

Although the afflicted lose control of their physical form, it is important to note that their spirit remains intact. Hence, the afflicted face struggles between the despair of physical bondage and the hope of spiritual liberation.[1] According to renowned exorcist Gabriele Amorth, possession exhibits distinct signs that distinguish it from other forms of demonic interference. One of the most noteworthy signs involves a corrupted form of the charismatic gift[2] of speaking in tongues, or "glossolalia." During a possession event, the afflicted often speak in languages that were previously unknown to them. These languages include ancient languages such as Aramaic, Sumerian, and Assyrian, as well as unidentifiable languages that some spiritualists such as Francoise Strachan have considered to be forms of demonic language. Regardless of the language, one constant is that the phenomenon is a tainted form of the charismatic gift of speaking in tongues, whereby the Holy Spirit descends upon the charismatic and speaks through them. This sacred event echoes the Acts of the Apostles, where the Holy Spirit descends upon the disciples and gives them the ability to speak in all tongues, a kind of reversal of the Fall of the Tower of Babel. In cases of possession, Satan or another demonic spirit descends upon the

---

[1] Francoise Strachan Casting Out Devils provides some excellent case studies in this area.

[2] Charismatic gifts are special abilities conferred on individuals who share a particularly strong connection with the divine, although they are more accurately means for the Holy Spirit to work through the charismatic as an instrument of God's Will.

individual, using them as a mouthpiece for their words of evil.

Demons: What They Are and Where They Come From

Demons come in a variety of forms, but they all share something in common: they come from a place beyond our human plane. Although they may interact with our physical world, they are primarily spiritual beings. The word "demon" itself has a complex history. Originally from the Greek, daimon (or δαίμων) meant "god-like," referring to spirits that were superhuman but not technically deities. This included nymphs, satyrs, and various monstrosities.[3] As this tradition was absorbed by Christianity, demons came to represent almost exclusively malevolent beings, most often agents of Satan. In the earliest Christian writings, especially the Pauline Epistles, the term "demon" most often distinguishes pagan deities from the Almighty. In his first letter to the Corinthians, Paul writes: "Consider the people of Israel; are not those who eat the sacrifices partners in the altar? What do I imply then? That food sacrificed to idols is anything, or that an idol is anything? No, imply that what pagans sacrifice, they sacrifice to demons and not to God. I do not want you to be partners with demons. You cannot drink from the cup of the Lord and the cup of demons.

---

[3] Interestingly, in Homer, daimon and theos are used almost interchangeably.

You cannot partake of the table of the Lord and the table of demons" (1 Cor 18-21). This early reference to demons as evil spirits carries throughout subsequent Church tradition.

Demons may spring from desecrated places both within and without. The internal source of the demonic is our human frailty, which allows Satan and his minions to enter our lives and exert their influence. The external source of the demonic is commonly described as Hell, that place furthest removed from God's grace. Yet Hell is not a place so much as a state of mind. As John Milton reminds us in Paradise Lost, "The mind is its own place, and in itself can make a heaven of hell, a hell of heaven." By remembering this truth, we can not only identify when evil enters our surroundings but also fortify ourselves with the knowledge that regardless of how dark our lives may get, the Light is never far so long as we gird ourselves with faith and love.

In contemporary Catholic demonology, the ranks of demons are an inversion of the ranks of the Heavenly Host. Just as there exist nine distinct choirs of angels—Angels, Archangels, Principalities, Virtues, Powers, Dominations, Thrones, Cherubim, and Seraphim—there also exist different classes of demons, although according to St. Thomas Aquinas, order is inherently against demonic nature as they are beings of chaos. One of the most comprehensive classifications of demons comes from Cornelius Agrippa's De Occulta Philosophia (1510), which classifies demons based on what he calls "scales."

The first scale, The Scale of Unity, includes only a single demon, Lucifer. The second, The Scale of Binary, contains Behemoth and Leviathan, both named in Revelation and listed as Chiefs of the Devils. The Scale of Ternary includes figures from Greek mythology considered demons, namely the Three Furies[4] and the Three Judges of Hades. The fourth, the Scale of Quaternary, includes Samael the Demon of Fire, Azazel the Demon of Air, Azael the Demon of Water, and Mahazael the Demon of Earth, as well four other Princes of Devils representing the four cardinal directions. The next level includes the Six Authors of All Calamities, powerful archdemons who appear in various traditions. Lastly, there is the Scale of Novenary, which includes the Nine Princes of Hell, each of which appears in Scripture: Beelzebub, the demon of False Idols (Matthew 4:1-11); Python, the demon of lies (1 Kings 22:21-22); Belial the demon of wrath (Genesis 49:5, Isaiah 13:5, Ezekiel 9:2); Asmodeus the demon of wickedness; Satan the demon of delusion (Genesis 3:1-5); Merihem the demon of aerial powers (Revelation 7:1-2); Abaddon the demon of mischief; Astaroth the demon of accusers; and Mammon the demon of temptation. Again, these lists vary by source, but one thing remains clear: demons come in many forms and differ in the level of power they can wield over mortals.

---

[4] Usually listed as Alecto, Megara, and Ctesiphon, but these names vary in classical sources such as Homer and Hesiod, as well as in later sources such as Dante. The three judges, however, are more or less consistent across texts.

Demons Exist Regardless of Religious Beliefs

Regardless of one's personal religious beliefs, demons exist among us. In nearly every cultural tradition, some form of malevolent spiritual being appears. As early as the Sumerian civilization, demons were depicted as beings from the underworld *Kur*. The evil spirits in Greek tradition, such as Furies, Harpies, and satyrs, share many features with demons, largely due to the Christian absorption of Greek culture after Paul's ministry to the gentile community in the first century. In Jewish tradition, demons were mostly adapted from pagan gods, such as the Canaanite god Baal who would later become Belial and Beelzebub in Christian demonology. Another Judaic tradition describes demons as the descendants of Lilith, the first wife of Adam who turned away from God. In Islam, the *jinn* were spirits that constantly troubled human beings. Among the most significant *jinn* was Shaitan, a clear parallel to Satan. Even the Buddhist tradition mentions demons as minions of Yama, the underworld—although perhaps most interestingly, in the Buddhist tradition, demons represent mental states more than external agents.

In some mystical traditions, demons are seen as a potential source of power. One of the earliest accounts of this is in the legend of King Solomon, who, in the Talmudic version, used demons to construct his grand temple.[5] Praised for his wisdom, Solomon decided to enslave a demon, Ashmedai (later equated with the demon prince Asmodeus in later literature), to build his temple. Another version in the Midrash—and retold in later medieval versions—claims that Solomon enslaved 72 lesser demons and the Seven Princes of Hell to complete his divine project using ten rings gifted to him by God in a dream. In all the versions, Solomon devised a glyph to protect himself from the demons' influence, his famous seal. The seal consisted of a hexagram surrounded by three magic circles containing words of power capable of controlling the demon's actions. The Seal of Solomon remains a powerful protective tool for modern practitioners of spiritual warfare and is especially cherished by Qabala.

A similar tale of demonic influence used for good comes from the Arthurian tradition, where in many versions the wizard Merlin is himself the son of a demon. One of the earliest of these accounts is Robert de Boron's poem Merlin, which begins with a plot by demons to create an Antichrist to undo the sacrifice of Christ.[6] However, Merlin's mother baptizes the child, leading to Merlin being a force of good rather than evil, culminating in his helping Arthur's knights find the Holy Grail. In this case, demonic interference inadvertently leads to positive outcomes, not unlike the accidental spiritual benefits of the Fall

---

[5] Kiperwasser, R. (2021). Solomon and Ashmedai Redux: Redaction Criticism of bGitin 68b. Jewish Quarterly Review 111(1), 21-54. doi:10.1353/jqr.2021.0002.
[6] Noted in many Arthurian sources, especially in Nikolai Tolstoy's The Quest for Merlin and the work of Geoffrey Ashe.

itself.

Both Solomon and Merlin remain exceptions rather than rules when it comes to human interactions with demonic forces. Stories of similar attempts to harness demonic power rarely end well. English playwright Christopher Marlowe's The Tragical History of the Life and Death of Doctor Faustus (1592) tells the story of one such attempt by an otherwise prudent scholar who makes a pact with the demon Mephistopheles. In exchange for his soul, Faust is given 24 years with the demon as his servant and the gift of magical powers. Of course, when his time draws near, Faust regrets his decision and is dragged from the stage toward eternal damnation by a pack of demons. The tale was later told by German Romantic Wolfgang von Goethe in Faust (1790), presenting Faust as a tragic hero rather than a villain, his true sin being pride. In both cases, Faust dabbles in powers beyond his understanding and pays the ultimate spiritual price.

How the Devil Seeks to Influence Us

The influence of Satan comes in many forms, some obvious, many subtle. The most devious interventions of the Adversary are those that convince us to turn against others or ourselves. Doubt is the devil's greatest weapon. By driving us toward disbelief in the power of the Divine, Satan makes us vulnerable to temptation and all falsehoods. We begin to believe that we are the center of the universe rather than a mere part of

Creation. We begin to turn against our partners in spiteful ways, even if they don't deserve it. We begin to doubt not only our self-worth but also our purpose, which leads us to, in turn, doubt God's purpose for us.

Even more deceitful is Satan's tendency to make us doubt his own existence. As the poet Charles Baudelaire famously announced, "The greatest trick the devil ever pulled was convincing the world he doesn't exist." In a similar vein, Lucien-Mary of St. Joseph more recently has said: "It is doubtless the masterpiece of this master of illusions to pass himself off as nonexistent in a world where he so easily gets souls to go the way he wants, without needing to show himself: He has every interest in not doing so" (95). In today's world, with so many people rejecting spirituality in favor of material gain, the Devil has made many people believe he is a myth, a relic of an outdated way of thinking. Pope Francis recently reminded the faithful of this unfortunate trend: "This generation, and many others, have been led to believe that the devil is a myth, a figure, an idea, the idea of evil…But the devil exists and we must fight against him." This is perhaps the Adversary's most devious strategy because if we deny the existence of Satan, we cannot recognize when he is working against us. This blindness to evil often results because Satan is cunning, not always announcing his plans or intentions. As the old Scottish proverb goes, "The devil's boots don't creak."

Often, the devil's voice can seem like our own insecurities trying to convince us to stray from the Light. This most often occurs through sin, a Hebrew word for "missing the mark." Whenever we sin, we drift further away from the Divine, the source of all Love, and draw closer to the Dark. The devil is, above all, a tempter, and he uses whatever means possible to deceive us into choosing the path of the flesh over that of the spirit. The Seven Deadly Sins, which in medieval theology were actual demonic beings, present the most severe forms of temptation. Pride tempts us to put ourselves above others and defy the Word. Envy tempts us to grow jealous of what others have. Wrath leads us to destructive acts, while Lust causes us to put sexual pleasure above all else. Greed convinces us that material possessions and financial gain are the most important things in life, leading us away from what truly matters. Sloth tempts us to put off our duties to family and community and instead waste our time in unproductive ways. All these forms of diabolical influence exist today, and each must be resisted if we are to grow spiritually. Protecting ourselves with the power of prayer and the might of the Word is the first and most important step to spiritual fulfilment.

According to Scripture, Satan and his minions operate through specific actions. Not only do they use misleading actions themselves, but they also attempt to sway us to commit these sins ourselves. Among the most prominent threats we face from demons are their tendency to lie (John 8:44) and deceive (1 Timothy 4:1). Satan is, among other things, the Father of Lies, determined to sow doubt and distrust among us. In the same way, Satan and his demons rely on our doubts to lure us into temptation (Matthew 4:1). This includes not only the Cardinal Sins discussed earlier but also the chaos and discord sowed by actions such as accusing (Zechariah 3:1) and corrupting (2 Peter 2:10-12). These actions are aimed at defiling God's work, and demons are experts at tempting us to do the same by creating conflict between us and others. By isolating us and creating strife, Satan makes us more vulnerable to his trickery and leads us toward all manner of destruction.

Two saints who give us special insight into the workings of Satan and his apostate angels are St. John of the Cross and St. Teresa of Avila, both skilled exorcists from the Spanish mystical tradition. Both note that often Satan "counterfeits God"[7] by presenting us with "false apparitions of saints, or in beautiful or apparently holy words."[8] This deception applies both to our outer and inner perceptions. "The devil often purveys objects to the senses, affording to the sense of sight images of saints and most beautiful lights…And to the sense of smell, fragrant odors; and he puts sweetness in one's mouth," writes St. John of the Cross. "He does all of this so that by enticing persons through these sensory objects he may induce them into many evils."[9] Similarly, St. Teresa of Avila notes throughout her writings how Satan and his agents often disguised themselves as

---

[7] Moreno, A. (2022). Demons according to St. Teresa and St. John of the Cross, in Catholic Culture
[8] Ibid.
[9] Ascent p. 133

holy figures, even appearing to her in the form of Christ.

Division is another means by which the devil seeks to influence our lives. As Sister Theresa Aletheia Noble puts it, "Division is one of the devil's favorite tools in his toolbox." Division implies both Satan's attempts to divide us from God personally as well as his deceptions that drive us apart from each other. Pitting wife against husband, brother against brother, mother against son are the work of satanic forces of division. According to St. Philip Neri, "Our enemy, the devil, who fights with us in order to vanquish us, seeks to disunite us in our houses, and to breed quarrels, dislikes, contests and rivalries because while we are fighting each other, he comes and conquers us and makes us more securely his own." In other words, when we lose focus and fix our aggressions on others, we lose sight of the devil's plots against us. Losing focus opens us up to sin, and as Origen of Alexandria noted, "Where there is division, there is sin." In this sense, the Enemy enhances his influence on us when we forget that all other enemies pale in comparison to him.

A final method used by the devil to influence us is exploiting our weaknesses. "Just as the commander of an army pitches his camp, studies the strength and defenses of a fortress, and then attacks it on its weakest side," St. Ignatius of Loyola once wrote regarding Satan, "in like manner, the enemy of our human nature studies from all sides our theological, cardinal, and moral virtues. Wherever he finds us weakest and most in need regarding our eternal salvation, he attacks and tries to take us by storm." As the founder of the Jesuit Order, a monastic order often referred to as the Soldiers of Christ, St. Ignatius meant that Satan quite literally operates by taking advantage of our weaknesses and shortcomings.

Understanding Different Kinds of Evil Curses

Although curses might seem like something archaic or obsolete, they are increasingly common even in today's technologically saturated world. According to one recent study, "curses are on the rise in western culture as people dabble more and more in the occult and in organizations where people take secret oaths" (Edmiston 2010). Curses come in many forms, but they are unequivocally evil in intent.[10] The most recent OED definition of "curse" reads thus: "a solemn utterance intended to invoke a supernatural power to inflict harm on someone or something." Like any spell, a curse is an intention, an act of will whereby we attempt to change something about reality.

Curses come in many forms, though, as Anne Marie Kitz notes, they all share a "grammar."[11] This grammar is a formula that

---

[10] Technically this statement is not necessarily always true, especially given the number of curses on behalf of God, especially in the Pentateuch and Psalms. Also, Paul repeatedly mentions that Christ himself is a curse, insofar as he became a curse against curses, while also being cursed as one "hanged from a tree."

[11] Kitz, A.M. "The Grammar of Curses." Cursed Are You! Penn State P, 2014. Note that she draws on Pederson, who denies that curses possess a performative

structures the curse itself, determining both target and outcome. As Sheldon H. Blank[12] noted in his seminal study of curses, the Bible depicts three forms of curse: simple, composite, and freely composed. The main distinctions are that simple and composite curses are both premeditated, with a specific objective in mind, whereas the third form is spurred more by impulse. The second distinction lay in the target of the curse itself. The simple curse is one directed toward a person, whereas the composite targets multiple people.[13] The desired outcome of the curse may or may not come about, though the intention remains the most important aspect.

Although several different categorizations of curses exist, the Catholic tradition identifies three primary types: generational, verbal, and occult. Generational curses are those that pass from parents to children and perhaps to subsequent generations. An early example of a generational curse appears in Exodus 36:7: "the iniquity of the fathers upon the children and the children's children to the third and the fourth generation." These types of curses are difficult to break, given that they transcend a single individual. One common theme, however, is that generational curses often begin with the sins of a parent leading to negative energy in their children's lives. If we think of Cain, we can see

---

dimension, which is problematic to say the least.

[12] Blank, S. H. (1950). The Curse, The Blasphemy, The Spell, and the Oath. Hebrew Union College Annual 23(1).

[13] It should be noted here that curses may also be directed at objects or even places. In addition, they are not necessarily always malevolent, as Christ's curse of the fig tree suggests in the Gospels (Matthew 21:18-22; Mark 11-14, 20-25). See also Benedict Kent's work on curses.

this kind of curse in action as his entire bloodline is cursed for his murder of his twin Abel. Similarly, Eve's eating of the forbidden fruit in Eden is a form of generational curse as all subsequent descendants of her and Adam bear the burden of Original Sin. We find a more recent famous literary example in Shakespeare's tragedy Romeo and Juliet, where the mortally wounded Mercutio cries, "A curse upon both your houses," a curse which ultimately comes true when the houses of Montague and Capulet effectively end with the suicides of Romeo and Juliet.

The second type of curse is the verbal curse, which can be written or oral. These curses draw their power from the words themselves and function opposite of blessings. Whereas blessings have a positive intention, verbal curses are rooted in malicious intent. As James 3:10 states, "Out of the same mouth proceed blessing and cursing. My brethren, these things ought not to be so." The verbal curse can apply to various situations, from curses of infertility to curses of physical harm. A notable example of the former comes in Shakespeare's King Lear when the king curses his treacherous eldest daughter Goneril: "I curse your organ of increase," a curse intended to render her sterile.

The last type of curse recognized in the tradition is the occult curse, a category that includes a wide range of spells. Occult curses are those that in the Biblical tradition are affiliated with dark magic and involve dabbling in powers not intended for human use. The Bible generally identifies these curses with sorcery and witchcraft, although we must remember that these blanket terms referred to any ritual outside of Judaic law. Later Christian tradition would likewise group these types of curses together. One frequent element in this type of curse is the use of a taglock, a term for material taken from the person intended to be the curse's target.

Curses in the Bible also include old taboos, many of which were dispelled by St. Paul the Apostle. In the early days of the Church, when the Apostles debated how to integrate the Mosaic Law into the New Covenant, Paul reminded them that faith in Christ replaced the old law, which he saw as a form of curse: "Christ redeemed us from the curse of the law by become a curse for us, for it is written: 'Cursed is everyone who is hung on a tree'" (Gal. 3:13-14). This sense of "curse" is common in Paul's writings and generally symbolizes old bondages cast away through Christ's sacrifice.

The Human Spirit and Lucifer

The battle for the human soul is the first conflict in the Bible. As God presents the newly formed Adam to the hosts of angels, he asks them to bow: all of them do except Lucifer. The most influential retelling of this story comes from John Milton, the great 17th century poet. As Milton notes, Lucifer's refusal is bound to his sense of entitlement. "Better to reign in Hell," Lucifer states, "than to serve in Heaven." Above all else, Lucifer is proud. This pride, one of the seven deadly sins, threatens everyone because it tempts us to place ourselves above others and even God Himself. Lucifer could not bring himself to believe that Adam, a mere man, was greater than he, one of God's favorite angels.

Lucifer's fall from grace lay at the heart of the struggle between good and evil within the human soul. Lucifer—from the Greek lukos and pheros or "light-bringer"—was initially a figure of good, representing the morning star and the hope of dawn. After his betrayal, however, he became Satan, or "the Adversary." In many ways, Lucifer's fall from grace echoes the risk we all face in the presence of darkness, whether that darkness be doubt, betrayal, or despair. The human spirit contains within itself the internal risk of following Lucifer's own path.

As sons of Adam and daughters of Eve, we should all be aware of this legacy. When Lucifer was cast out of Heaven by Michael and the Heavenly Host, he did not remain idle. Instead, he concocted a plan to taint his Maker's work. As recounted in Genesis, Satan entered the Garden of Eden as a serpent and tempted Eve to eat the forbidden fruit from the Tree of Knowledge, forever cursing humanity. According to Catholic tradition, we are all born tainted with Original Sin, the mark of Eve's first betrayal of God in Eden. Only through the sacrament of Baptism can this Sin be cleansed, allowing us to experience God's grace purified of Satan's influence once again. This first step of cleansing provides our firmest foundation against the influence of demonic forces. Indeed, any type of purification ritual that reaffirms our trust in the Light protects us from demonic interference.

Ironically, Lucifer's attempt to corrupt God's work only served to reinforce what he sought to destroy, a result often referred to as the felix culpa, or "happy fall." By tempting Eve to betray God and eat the forbidden fruit, Satan inadvertently paved the way for human salvation by exercising free will and ultimate salvation through the sacrifice of Christ on the Cross. This unexpected turn of events partly fuels Satan's continual battle for our souls—in his pride, the Evil One cannot bear to admit defeat. Even when he believed he had finally achieved revenge after the Fall, Christ undid his work through a supreme act of love for humankind.

Today, it is especially important to recognize that Satan is not only real, but actively working against us. In That Evil Which is Called the Devil, Pope Paul VI noted that the faithful need to acknowledge the existence of personal evil as the work of Satan. Whether we are aware of it or not, the devil is constantly trying to work through us. He wants us to fail, wants us to doubt, wants us to abandon God so that we can lose our connection with grace. Of course, he can only achieve these goals if we let him into our hearts and turn away from the source of all positive energy, which is the Creator Himself.

The Human Spirit and Jesus

The human spirit does not exist alone and by virtue of Christ's sacrifice, can never truly die. One of the more dramatic episodes of medieval Christian "folklore" is the Harrowing of Hell. Although only briefly mentioned in Scripture, the moment of Christ's death on the Cross coincided with his breaching the Gates of Hell and freeing the Damned while also guaranteeing the salvation of the world as Salvator Mundi. This reversal of the First War—when Lucifer and his angels attempted to overthrow God out of pride and jealousy—positions Christ in the same position as Gilgamesh, Theseus, Hercules, and other heroes of pagan mythology who successfully stormed the Underworld and returned victorious. In the same way, Christ demonstrates his supreme power at this moment as the Son of God, humiliating Satan after so many failed attempts to tempt him (in the desert and perhaps most famously at Gethsemane). By crashing the Gates of Hell, Christ not only denies any power to Satan but also ensures us that even the worst sinners among us can still achieve salvation.

Our spiritual well-being relies on our relationship with the Creator, our ability to humble ourselves even as we attempt to be more like his Son, the paragon of all human virtue. This fact itself, as Thomas Aquinas, Francis of Assisi, and other revered saints have suggested, represents the most important aspect of faith itself—our belief in the Everlasting within ourselves and the hope that death is not the end so long as we accept Christ as our Savior. This submission is not confined to Christianity, of course. Any truly spiritual person fundamentally understands that they exist by the mercy of the greater powers, the Many in One, the Divine.

In matters of spiritual warfare, this understanding equips us with the fundamental toolkit for combatting evil interference. In the Rite of Major Exorcism, for example, the mere statement of one's belief in Christ is often enough to drive the possessing spirit into tantrums. These fits are among the first signs in a spiritual battle that the faithful hold the upper hand. In both Catholic and Orthodox traditions, the power to expel evil forces is given to the exorcist; however, many other traditions exist where the exorcist draws power from other sources, such as the will of the practitioner, forces of nature, or other benevolent spirits. Even in these rites, the power of good ultimately finds its source in the Creator. As Joseph Campbell notes in The Hero With a Thousand Faces, one of the most fascinating things about human spiritual traditions is that they share a remarkable number of similarities. This unity in diversity lends even more weapons to our arsenal in the spiritual battle between good and evil, regardless of which form they take.

The Process of Possession

Possession is not an event so much as a process. In the early stages, signs may be so subtle that they are mistaken for something else, such as emotional instability. As mentioned earlier, the signs of possession do not appear all at once, but in phases. The first part of the process is behavioral changes that cannot be explained by the environment or other causes. At this point, the afflicted individual may be facing several possible forms of demonic interference, including obsession, influence, or possession. All three of these forms involve changes in behavior that cause onlookers to recognize something is wrong. Oftentimes, these changes take the form of vocal outbursts, physical violence, and personality changes. At this stage, the demonic force is trying to take over the victim's body. Depending on the person's spiritual strength, this process can vary in time, with spiritually equipped individuals often able to resist possession longer than those with little spiritual ammunition.

One common strategy used by demons during possessions is to deceive the afflicted person into believing they are not harmful. According to Adam Christian Blai,[14] a prominent peritus—or theological consultant on demonology—for the Archdiocese of Pittsburgh, Pennsylvania, these deceptions usually come in the form of their appearance as a deceased loved one, an angel, or an innocent spirit that appears as a child. This approach tends to lower any defenses the individual might have against evil intentions. Second, Blai notes that demons tempt the afflicted

---

[14] Blai has recently published Hauntings, Possessions, and Exorcisms through Emmaus Road Press. He previously wrote A Roman Catholic Pastoral Manual for Exorcism, Deliverance, and Home Cases, a guidebook exclusively available for priests training to perform exorcisms.

with promises, usually related to some need in that person's life. For example, if the afflicted is facing financial difficulty, the demon will promise financial success. If the afflicted is confronted with marriage difficulties, they will promise love or a way out of their bond. Regardless of the promise, the words themselves are hollow because the demon is merely luring the individual deeper into their grasp, weakening their psychological and spiritual defenses so they can commandeer their victim's physical body.

The possession reaches the next phase when the individual has completely lost the voluntary use of their bodies. They are no longer in control because the demonic influence has now assumed control. At this point, the individual often begins to show signs of physical harm, such as bruises, burns, scratches, and in extreme cases, stigmata. The stigmata in possession cases, as Gabriele Amorth notes, are exceptionally rare, but they often indicate the most serious demonic forces are involved— including Satan himself. The presence of stigmata among saints such as St. Francis of Assisi symbolized the grace of God and a closeness to Christ; in the possessed, these marks on the hands and feet are a mockery of Christ's sacrifice.

The final stage in the possession process involves unexplainable phenomena around the afflicted person. These bizarre events include floating or moving objects, which show that the demon is using the body to channel its supernatural abilities. Levitation is another sign of the final stage that Amorth and other exorcists have described as a mockery of Christ walking on water in the Sea of Galilee. At this point in the process, the demonic entity not only controls the possessed person's body but also begins to infect the surroundings, much like in cases of demonic infestation. Nevertheless, despite the complete loss of control, the afflicted person's soul remains intact—and it is this sacred soul that provides the exorcist with the hope of liberating them from demonic control.

Demons or Mental Health Issues?

The issue of whether demonic interference is the result of spiritual disruptions or mental health issues remains a central concern of any practitioner. As Milton writes in Paradise Lost, "The mind is its own place, and in itself can make a heaven of hell, a hell of heaven." The signs and symptoms of possession and other forms of demonic interference share many similarities with mental health issues. A child may begin acting out violently, but does that necessarily mean they are possessed? A man may commit a heinous crime, but does that necessarily mean he did so under the influence of a demonic force? A woman may be convinced that she is being persecuted by an evil entity, but could she merely be struggling with delusions and hallucinations? All these questions are important to ask at the outset of any encounter with potential demonic interference.

In the medieval period, demonic possession was much more

commonly documented than it is today. This partly has to do with the lack of understanding about mental health issues such as schizophrenia, depression, and bipolar disorder, all of which were commonly identified as demonic possession rather than mental disorders. The medieval medical arts relied on diagnosing patients based on variations in their humors: phlegm, yellow bile (or cholic), black bile (or melancholia), and blood. Based on the work of ancient physician Hippocrates, this system dominated medicine for almost two thousand years until the rise of modern science began to replace it with evidence-based clinical investigation and experimental results. In the case of mental illness, most patients were diagnosed with imbalances in the humors, especially black bile. In extreme cases, when medical interventions such as bloodletting or leeching failed to yield any results, the patient was turned over to the Church. Oftentimes, the individual in question was not in fact under any kind of demonic influence and therefore exorcism was not an appropriate treatment. As a result, when exorcism failed to cure the afflicted, these individuals were isolated into communities and cast out from society. The most famous example of this is the Ship of Fools, where these outcasts were put on ships and set out to sea.[15]

As the Age of Reason paved the way for the rise of experimental science, mind diseases fell under the new field of psychology. First introduced by Wilhelm Wundt and William James, the field

---

[15] Foucault's work on The Ship of Fools in The Birth of the Clinic and his work on madness remains among the best explanations of why this inhumane treatment still exists in some form in the modern mental institution.

was brought to wider attention by Sigmund Freud, whose work in psychoanalysis revolutionized science even though it drew many critics. Freud's own work involved many cases of patients who would have been identified as "possessed" or "demoniacal" in earlier times, but throughout his case studies, he determined that many suffered from neurosis, not supernatural interference. As B. F. Skinner demonstrated the important role of conditioning in behavior, other advancements in psychiatry also began to identify cases of possession as instead mental illness. Many skeptics in the psychological and psychiatric communities, such as Emil Kraepelin, Nathan S. Kline,[16] and Aaron Beck, largely dismissed possession as a severe form of mental illness. At the same time, modern behavioral science has failed to completely explain the bizarre occurrences in cases of demonic interference, as many of the signs cannot be accounted for by mental dysfunction. To truly grasp the threat of demonic interference in the physical realms, we must recognize the fundamental differences between mental health issues and demonic interference—in doing so, better arming ourselves against any form of negative interference, whether cognitive or spiritual.

As work by Michel Foucault, Jacques Lacan, and others have suggested, the demonic represents a spectrum of phenomena, many of which belong to the realm of the psychiatric rather than ecclesiastic. In The Birth of the Clinic and Madness and

---

[16] Kline's Storming the Gates of Bedlam is a great source of his clinical career and his revolutionary use of psychiatric medication to treat mental patients in the 20th century.

Civilization, Foucault outlines a major cultural shift in the West from "leper colonies" to "sanitaria," a practical institutional shift away from leper colony to asylum. This shift coincided with a change in thinking among psychiatrists themselves, from ostracizing to humanizing, from "cast them out" to "isolate and medicate." One of the major proponents of this approach was Dr. Nathan S. Kline, who revolutionized mental health treatment by introducing increased use of medication in treatment. Another great advance arrived with Aaron Beck's development of cognitive behavioral therapy, which, combined with pharmacological treatment, remains one of the most successful forms of psychiatric treatment. In all these instances, the change was based on focusing on the patient as an individual rather than on their insanity. As Carl Rogers, the renowned developer of humanistic or client-centered psychology, noted, the goal of treating the mentally ill is to restore the patient's personhood as much as it is addressing the symptoms of their condition.

To truly determine whether the problem is mental or spiritual, we must ask certain questions. Does this individual have a prior history of mental illness? Have they sought any treatment from mental health professionals such as therapists, psychologists, or psychiatrists? Are they currently being medicated for any mental health issues? Do they have a history of psychological trauma? If the afflicted fits into any of these categories, we must be sure to proceed carefully.

On the one hand, demonic interference can occur in those also suffering from mental illness. On the other hand, the symptoms of the two are oftentimes so similar that it can be difficult to distinguish one from the other. The classic case of this difficulty is schizophrenia, a mental condition characterized by disordered thought processes, auditory and visual hallucinations, and other symptoms. In many cases, these symptoms were often confused with possession. For example, patients with schizophrenia often claim to hear voices, a symptom once mistaken for demonic interference. Similarly, major depression in severe cases can lead to suicide, which for many years was identified as a result of demonic obsession.

According to the most recent Vatican protocols, psychiatric and psychological tests must be run before the bishop can approve an exorcism. Multiple professionals must evaluate the afflicted person to determine beyond doubt that the problem is spiritual and not mental. Only after all other possibilities are ruled out can the bishop formally permit an exorcism. In recent years, priests undergoing training to perform exorcisms are also trained in mental healthcare, giving them the added skill set needed to distinguish between mental illness and spiritual sickness.

External Solicitation Toward Evil and Negativity

Solicitation to evil stems from both internal and external forces. Not only are diabolical forces constantly at work to divert us from our paths and corrupt our souls, but our innate human weakness also poses a threat. Again, the legacy of Eden haunts us, a memory these forces try to exploit again and again if we are not properly prepared to summon our faith and defend ourselves. The Fall tainted our souls, and even though baptism cleanses of that Original Sin, the Tempter refuses to give up his battle for our souls. We are constantly at the center of a cosmic war between the forces of good and evil, with our souls as the real weapons. When we choose to side with the Light, we deprive the Adversary of ammunition. He wants to damn as many souls as he can, each one a small victory over his Maker. For this reason, there is no tactic that Satan won't use in his attempt to seduce us toward evil.

At the same time, demons present us with challenges from outside ourselves. Part of this comes from what theologians call "the mystery of iniquity." This problem arises from the question of why some angels, with all their gifts, powers, and nearness to the Divine, should choose the demonic path. If even angels could fall victim to these kinds of temptation, what hope do we have as mere mortals? As noted in the Second Epistle of Peter, "And the angels which kept not their first estate but left their own habitation he hath reserved in everlasting chains under darkness" (2 Pet 2). These demons, cast from Heaven, are nonetheless able to enter our world. The story of Satan's fall from grace also notes that he goes by many names: "And the great dragon was cast out, that old Serpent called the Devil and Satan which deceiveth the whole world; he was cast out into the earth and his angels were cast out with him" (Jude 6). The symbolism of the serpent, cursed to crawl on its belly in humility, reflects the pride which cost Satan his place beside the Throne of God.

Indeed, Satan's hatred towards human beings is rooted in his own pride, which itself stems from doubt, both in himself and in his Creator. Despite his apparent victory in Eden, Satan ultimately lost the war when Christ washed away the world's sins with the ultimate sacrifice, "For God so loved the world that he gave his only begotten son" (1 Cor 29). The external solicitation to evil is therefore rooted in Satan's persistence to undo the work of God at all costs. This may come in the form of influence from others acting under the influence of Satan, or it may come from our own submission in the face of difficulties in our lives. Whatever the cause, the result is the same: we fall farther from Grace and closer toward the risk of losing the most precious gift of all: our soul.

Internal Solicitation to Evil and Negativity

The internal solicitation of evil is a bit less obvious. First, there is the risk of our own fallen nature. Yet this very fallen nature is the source of our free will, which itself is what distinguishes us from angels. Because we are free to choose between good and evil, our choices are more significant. In turn, we face the risk of temptation, perhaps the most powerful weapon in the demonic arsenal. Temptation comes in many forms, of course, but it almost always involves one of the Seven Deadly Sins. For example, we may be tempted by the beauty of another man's wife, and even if we do not act on it, we submit to Lust. Adultery may seem like an external solicitation given that another person is involved, but in truth, the temptation to act on our lustful thoughts is an internal solicitation that leads to destructive consequences. Infidelity breaks homes, wrecks trust, and shatters love. These consequences produce negative energy in all the lives involved.

Other internal solicitations follow a similar pattern. We may be tempted to anger, allowing Wrath a victory over us. We may prioritize material possessions over more important things such as our family, giving Greed power over us. We may waste our time when we could be doing positive work, leading Sloth to dominate us. In all these instances, we fail ourselves because we lack the power to resist temptation. Each of these Sins is itself a powerful demon, and each can intervene in our lives unexpectedly. By the time we are aware that we have fallen under the influence of these demonic forces, the damage may already be done. Yet, with meditative practice rooted in Scripture combined with a resolve to undo the demonic damage, we can always redeem ourselves. Forgiveness remains the core of the power within the Catholic tradition, one that can strengthen us regardless of our faith or creed.

In his Letter to the Galatians, St. Paul reminds us that internal solicitations to evil often stem from the temptations of sinful acts: "The acts of the sinful nature are obvious: sexual immorality, impurity, and debauchery; idolatry and witchcraft; hatred, discord, jealousy, fits of rage, selfish ambition, dissensions, factions, and envy; drunkenness, orgies, and the like. I warn you, as I did before, that those who live like this will not inherit the kingdom of God" (Gal 5: 19-21). Paul's list includes many of the Seven Deadly Sins (lust, envy, wrath), but also many of the behaviors condemned by God in the Law of Moses, such as idolatry. We should also note here that Paul's warning against witchcraft more accurately refers to occult practices which use unholy supernatural forces or dark magic, not practices using the Divine as a conduit for benevolent effect.

Most importantly, internal solicitations often come through our own human frailty. Remember, Satan wants to exploit our weaknesses. As St. Thomas Aquinas notes in Summa Theologica, the devil is not the cause of our sins so much as our own shortcomings, and Satan is always an opportunist when we fail. St. Teresa of Avila makes a similar point in The Foundations. When our will is weak, when our faith waivers, that is when Satan is most likely to strike. In many ways, will is our primary defense against such internal solicitations. "The devil is like a rabid dog tied to a chain," St. Padre Pio wrote, "beyond the length of the chain, he cannot seize anyone. And you: keep at a distance. If you approach too near, you let yourself be caught. Remember that the devil has only one door by which to enter the soul: the will." St. Padre Pio, who himself suffered diabolic attacks throughout his life, makes an important point here by reminding us that the will must remain strong in all instances of spiritual warfare.

Challenges of Demonic Access

Many barriers exist that prevent demonic access. Faith is perhaps the first line of defense in this case. St. Teresa of Avila repeatedly notes this in her writings, emphasizing what St. Paul the Apostle claims throughout Scripture: the supreme power of faith against evil. As St. Teresa states of Satan, "God will not permit him to deceive a soul which has not trust whatever in itself and is strengthened by faith."[17] Emboldening ourselves

with our belief in the Divine—regardless of by which name we call it—provides us with a shield against Satanic influence. This barrier requires nothing but our acknowledgment of our Creator's supreme place in the cosmos, the very type of submission which Satan could not bring himself to practice in

---

[17] Life, p. 238.

his pride. Simultaneously, faith requires that we resist Satan since he can only truly infiltrate us if we lower our defenses. As St. Francis de Sales once said, "Let the enemy rage at the gate; let him knock, pound, scream, howl; let him do his worst. We know for certain that he cannot enter our soul except by the door of our consent." If we lose focus, if we fall victim to sin, we risk opening this door and making ourselves more vulnerable. "The devil doesn't sit idly by while you seek God," Mark Hart writes, "If you're pursuing Christ, the enemy is pursuing you."

Baptism provides the first line of defense against demonic access. The ritual cleansing of our souls with holy water frees us from the burden of Original Sin and allows us to pursue redemption. Originating with the Judaic practice of mikveh, or ritual bathing for purification, Baptism follows an ancient tradition of spiritual cleansing through water (Leviticus 14-15). The sacrament itself mirrors John the Baptist immersing his cousin Jesus in the River Jordan, an event where the Holy Spirit itself descended from the heavens and decreed for those present that Jesus was, in fact, the Messiah who would wash away the sins of the world. When we participate in Baptism, we not only absolve ourselves of Adam and Eve's first transgression but also acknowledge that no matter how much we sin, forgiveness is always available to us. This eternal divine love protects us from demonic access using one of the most fundamental elements, water. As a symbol of purification, water is also the natural enemy of fire, the element of Hell. Any ritual intended to protect ourselves from demonic interference should involve water, especially holy water blessed by a clergy member. However, any blessing over water increases its potency against demons.

The second most powerful challenge to demonic access is prayer. Prayer can take many forms, though the most powerful is Scripture. The Word of God as written in these sacred texts is enough to repel most evil spirits. Other prayers are also effective, including the Hail Mary, the Lord's Prayer, and invocations to the saints. In the Major Rite of Exorcism, the mightiest weapon the exorcist can wield against the possessing demonic spirit is reading from Scripture and calling upon the Trinity to expel that evil. Prayer can also take the form of sacred medals, inscriptions, and even the Good Book itself, each of which contain within them the power of the words themselves. A Bible in the home has long been a mainstay of defense against demonic interference. Similarly, a crucifix in the home serves as a deterrent, a symbol of divine sacrifice and love, which demons find repulsive.

Prayer and faith together have the potential to lead us toward what Catholic mystics have called "the Seventh Mansion," a state of extreme union with God that offers protection from diabolical influence. This state of supreme grace allows those who achieve it to dispel demonic activity through their presence alone. According to their writings and Church doctrine, both St. John of the Cross and St. Teresa of Avila achieved this union with God. In both cases, their spiritual battles with Satan ended. Near the end of his Spiritual Canticle, John of the Cross finds himself relieved that Aminadab—his term for the satanic presence afflicting him for much of his life—never appeared again, repelled by the saint's holiness. Likewise, after achieving the Seventh Mansion, St. Teresa of Avila declared that demons "seem to be afraid of me. I have acquired an authority over them, bestowed upon me by the Lord of all, so that they are no more trouble to me; now they fly."[18] Of course, not all of us will become saints, even though striving to become one is in our best spiritual interest. Yet saints show us that there exist rare challenges to demonic access bestowed upon those with special spiritual attunement to the Divine.

Here it is again worth noting charismatic gifts of the Holy Spirit. First mentioned by St. Paul in his Epistles (1 Corinthians 12:4-11; Romans 12: 6-8), these gifts are unique capabilities bestowed by the Holy Spirit on individuals to fulfill a specific purpose. In some ways, those with charismatic gifts are instruments of the Divine, through which the Holy Spirit works. These gifts are not requested by the gifted, nor do they necessarily mean that the gifted individual is somehow holier than another. Instead, those blessed with charismatic gifts are meant to use them to enact the Holy Spirit's benevolent power. As the common saying goes, God works in mysterious ways, and the purpose of charismatic gifts is not always clear to those who possess them. However, in times of spiritual crisis—and especially when

---

[18] Life, p. 242.

confronted by demonic presences—charismatic gifts can provide extremely effective protection against evil. These gifts include the gift of healing, the gift of prophecy, the gift of tongues, the gift of discernment, the gift of mercy, the gift of teaching, and the gift of miracles. These gifts can prove useful in spiritual warfare, depending on a given circumstance. For example, someone with the charismatic gift of discernment has a preternatural ability to determine whether a person in crisis is facing a demonic presence or some other negative influence. Similarly, a person with the charismatic gift of healing can be supremely useful if the afflicted individual faces physical ailments brought on by demonic causes.

Other challenges to demonic access include sacred spaces. Although we will discuss these in more detail in Part 3, it is important to note that sacred spaces provide us with protection against demons in many circumstances. Any consecrated ground—whether a chapel, church, cathedral or even graveyard—protects us against demonic attack. The sacred energy coursing through these places repels evil in all its forms. As with sacred water, sacred places do not necessarily have to be Christian. Places sacred to the old gods often still have power, so long as the spirits have good intentions.

A final challenge to demonic access is one that receives less attention than it should: supplications to our ancestors. By calling upon our loved ones who have passed on before us, we can draw upon their power. As spirits close to us personally, they grant us a special sacred strength. This technique has a long tradition, as nearly all cultures throughout history have venerated their ancestors as protective spirits. In traditions such as Shinto, this is the primary defense against evil interference, and the Buddhist tradition has a long history of similar practice. In Western tradition, ancestors are often invoked in prayer, and in many folk traditions they serve as guardian spirits, similar to guardian angels. Like angels, our ancestors are always with us— no matter how isolated they may make us feel, demons never face a single soul since we are never truly alone.

PART 2

Demonic & Spiritual Warfare

Healing with Spiritual Warfare

Using spiritual warfare as a method of healing might seem at first contradictory. After all, warfare implies destruction rather than healing. However, demonic interference often leaves significant wounds even after the presence is cast out. To heal these wounds, we must understand that the victim requires compassion and further action. Casting out the demonic force is insufficient to prevent future attacks, nor does it entirely remove the stain of contact with evil forces.

Faith-healing has a long tradition in Christianity. By calling upon God's grace to heal sickness, faith-healing shows that the spiritual can and does affect the physical positively. The laying of hands is a common ritual associated with faith healing, as is the use of blessed artifacts such as medals, chrism (holy oil), holy water, crucifixes, and bibles. Incidentally, all these practices are also used in spiritual warfare when confronting an evil presence afflicting a person. The same principles apply. First, the faith of those present is capable of literally summoning the presence of grace into the space involved, whether that presence is the Holy Spirit, Christ, or a heavenly messenger such as a saint or angel. Second, the act of prayer itself forms a barrier, with each incantation accompanied by its own power. Third, the use of symbols is a powerful way to make the abstract concepts of the sacred mysteries into a tangible tool against the influence of evil.

The link between spiritual warfare and healing has strong Biblical roots, especially in the Gospels. In fact, remarkable parallels can be seen in the Synoptic Gospels (Mark, Matthew, and Luke) in this regard. When Jesus sends the Apostles out from Galilee, he grants them the gifts of healing both spiritual and physical ailments, these gifts almost always being granted together. In Matthew 10:1, we read that "when He had called His twelve disciples to Him, He gave them power over unclean spirits, to cast them out, and to heal all kinds of sickness and all kinds of disease." The gift of healing in Scripture is almost always capable of tackling physical illness and demonic forces. A similar account occurs in Luke 9:1 where we read that "He called His twelve disciples together and gave them power and authority over all demons, and to cure diseases. He sent them to preach the kingdom of God and to heal the sick." The earliest Apostolic missions were a combination of preaching and healing, the latter always a combination of curing bodily injuries and disease as well as confronting the various agents of Satan afflicting the people of Galilee and beyond. For this reason, spiritual warfare is necessarily a form of healing tied to physical faith healing. Often, it's difficult to distinguish where physical infirmity ends and spiritual decay begins in cases where demonic influence is strong.

Different Approaches to Exorcism

There are a variety of approaches to exorcism depending on the tradition involved. The approach most familiar to laypeople comes from the Catholic tradition, a practice known as the *Rituale Romanum*. More commonly called the "Roman Catholic Rite" (or "RC Rite"), this approach was made famous in the film *The Exorcist* but involves much more than the sensationalized film depicts. In fact, the history of the *Rituale Romanum* dates back to the 7th century, when St. Alcuin added an appendix known as the Gelasianum to the Gregorianum and the Ordines.[19] This appendix included prayers specifically intended to equip priests with prayers and blessings capable of driving off demonic forces. The first full version of a text intended to provide readers with defenses and weapons for these encounters was commissioned by Pope Paul V in 1614, a version later updated by Pope Benedict XIV in 1742 and again

---

[19] These are sacramentaries which include the well-known Gregorian Chants, as well as supplemental prayers for both public and private services.

by Pope Leo XIII in 1884, a version which more or less remained unchanged until more recent revisions in 1976. This ritual involves specific formulas of prayers and ritual actions to cast out a demonic presence.

Although certainly the most popular form of exorcism, the Catholic Major Rite of Exorcism is by no means the only approach. A similar practice exists in the Anglican and Episcopalian traditions, using different texts with often identical symbolic actions. Pentecostalists often call upon the Holy Spirit to cast out the evil spirit. This practice comes from the Acts of the Apostles when the Holy Spirit descended upon the apostles doubting Christ's resurrection. Versions of these approaches can also be found in the Voodoo traditions of Haitian and Cajun culture, where exorcism is a complex interaction between the possessed, the exorcist, and intercessory spirits, including saints, gods, and occasionally other demons.

Consolation and Desolation[20]

Perhaps two of the most important terms for our spiritual arsenal are consolation and desolation. These terms represent opposite spiritual directions, the first toward and the second away from God's grace. With consolation, we find ourselves

---

[20] These terms are generally considered to originate in the Ignatian tradition but have found their way into a variety of other traditions, both Catholic and Protestant. A great resource for these two forces as seen in contemporary theological practice is the work of Margaret Silf, a professor at Loyola University.

embracing higher levels of faith, experiencing more hope, and witnessing more love in ourselves and others. These forces also provide powerful protection against demonic interference. In many ways, consolation comes from practicing not only the words of Christ and the saints but also from living a Christ-like life. This approach can include literal ways of imitating Christ— such as St. Augustine's lifestyle after his conversion in Confessions or St. Francis of Assisi's attempts to embody Christ's devotion to poverty, charity, and compassion—or a more internal spiritual attempt to embrace one's Christ-likeness, as Thomas à Kempis famously outlined in his still-popular 15th century devotional The Imitation of Christ. In both cases, the devoted aims to embrace the Holy Spirit and come closer to a sense of oneness with the divine, especially through a personal relationship with Christ.

Desolation, on the other hand, represents the opposite direction. This term describes moving away from God and his Grace. Signs of desolation include anger, doubt, anxiety, selfishness, and a general sense of hopelessness. All these signs also appear in cases of demonic possession precisely because the afflicted is moving away from God, usually against their own will. In many instances, desolation is a downward spiral that is difficult to escape. Doubt leads us to isolate ourselves, leading to more depression and anger. We begin to feel less happy in our hobbies, relationships, and careers. In effect, we begin to lose a sense of joy because we are drifting away from the supreme source of joy, the divine.

Ebbs and Flows of Consolation and Desolation

It is important to note that consolation and desolation are not mutually exclusive; that is, we are rarely entirely in one state or the other. In fact, throughout our lives, even the most devout among us will inevitably drift from consolation to desolation. Only when we focus on strengthening our relationship with the Divine can we hope to overcome the gloomy swamp of desolation and re-enter the light of Grace. How can we accomplish this? One way is to focus beyond our own needs, through charitable actions and compassion towards those around us. This includes addressing the needs of our community through outreach, teaching our families the virtues of good work, and taking the time to shut out the hectic modern world and listen to the divine within us. These simple daily practices can help us strengthen our voice and regain a stronger connection with God, equipping us to cope with potential demonic interferences in our lives and those of others.

The Voices of God and Satan

Distinguishing between the voices of God and Satan is one of the major paths between consolation and desolation. At first, this might seem like a simple task: God's voice is good, whereas

Satan's voice is evil. However, the Evil One is also a Trickster.[21] His honeyed words are capable of deceiving us into believing that he speaks the truth, especially when he preys on our spiritual doubts. He can also mimic the voice of God. As Shakespeare noted in The Merchant of Venice:

"The devil can cite Scripture for his purpose.

An evil soul producing holy witness

Is like a villain with a smiling cheek,

A goodly apple rotten at the heart.

O, what a goodly outside falsehood hath"

Shakespeare is pointing to a fundamental truth held by both Catholic and Protestant traditions that Satan often uses God's words to lead us astray. This can also be true of his servants, as demons are known to be masterful liars.

At the same time, the Voice of God transcends all others. No matter how dire a given circumstance, true faith in God's Word and supplication to his goodness can help deliver us from every evil. The power of discernment, often listed among the great charismatic gifts in the Christian tradition, allows us to

---

[21] There are tons of parallels between Satan/Lucifer and Trickster figures in various traditions, especially as noted by Frazer's work in The Golden Bough, Joseph Campbell's wide-ranging work on monomyths, and Robert Graves's masterpieces The White Goddess, King Jesus, and his work on the Hebrew Myths.

distinguish the benevolent Voice of God from the deceitful voice of Satan. In any situation, if we quiet our spirits sufficiently to hear the Heavenly Host, we cannot be led astray except through our own weakness. Even then, the infinite power of forgiveness frees us from our own human frailty and empowers us to resist temptation.

Discerning Good and Bad Spirits

So how can we distinguish between good and bad spirits? What qualities differentiate them? For one, good spirits will lead us toward consolation, whereas bad spirits will inevitably lead us toward desolation. For another, good spirits tend toward truth while bad spirits lend themselves to falsehood and deceit. As we discussed in our treatment of Satan's tactics, discerning between good and evil spirits raises difficulties because of the demonic tendency to deceive us into believing they are holy. To discern between them requires focus, intuition, and spiritual awareness: "A person, in consequence, will have to be very spiritual to recognize this" (St. John of the Cross, Ascent, p. 207).

As noted in John 4:1-3, "Beloved, believe not every spirit, but try the spirits whether they are of God: because many false prophets are gone out into the world." This points to a valuable technique for discerning good from evil: testing them. Similarly, in 1 Timothy 4:1, we are taught that "the Spirit speaketh expressly, that in the latter times some shall depart from the

faith, giving heed to seducing spirits, and doctrines of devils."
In today's turbulent times, it is easy to fall into despair about the
many afflictions facing the world, especially how these may or
may not be, in part, the result of demonic interference. One of
the primary tools against this despair is maintaining faith in the
benevolence of the divine and reminding ourselves that not all
calamities are the result of otherworldly forces.

Another tool for discerning between spirits who mean harm to
do us harm and those helpful to us is through the charismatic
gift of discernment. As we discussed earlier, charismatic gifts are
special abilities bestowed upon the select faithful so that they
might act as instruments for the Holy Spirit. One of these gifts
is the power of discernment, in which the charismatic can
determine the nature of a given spirit or detect the presence of
one. Many practicing exorcists are themselves charismatics,
often with the power of discernment, but charismatics might
also be lay people or even, in rare cases, those outside the faith
altogether. In confrontations with the demonic, however, the
status of the charismatic is far less important than the gift itself.
Through their special connection with the Holy Spirit,
charismatics with the gift of discernment can act as effective
detectors of demonic energy. In cases where mental disability
remains a possibility, a charismatic person with this gift can
often confirm or deny the involvement of a demonic entity. Of
course, demons are often aware when they are in the presence
of such gifts of the Holy Spirit, and they will stop at nothing to
convince those around them to doubt the gifts. Yet discernment

stands as one of the best tools available to us for this aspect of spiritual warfare.

Satan and the Fallen Angels

At the same time, one can hardly deny that demonic interference lurks behind our lives, lying in wait like a wolf in winter. The most powerful demonic forces include Satan and those angels who fell with him after refusing to prostrate before Adam. This led to a battle in Heaven in which the Archangel Michael cast Satan and his armies into the abyss known as Hell, Sheol[22], or Tartarus.

In many cases, the demons involved in cases of possessions are one of Satan's generals. For example, St. Nicholas of Tolentino—a noted worker of miracles—suffered for years from physical injuries due to demonic interference. As his biographer noted, the demon later identified himself as Belial, one of Satan's most powerful minions: "I am Belial, and I have been sent to you as a prod for your holiness." This struggle with demonic influence from even the holiest among us shows that the demonic can afflict any of us, regardless of our faith.

Again, the most well-known account for this comes from

---

[22] Sheol is the most common name for the Underworld or Land of the Dead in the Judaic tradition, found at points in the Torah, as well as in the Mishnah, Midrash, and Talmud.

Milton's Paradise Lost, where he recounts in great detail from the Christian tradition the battle for Heaven and its inevitable result in the Original Sin. Even though they were defeated, as retold in Revelation 12:19, the fallen angels never stop in their quest to pervert and defile God's work, especially human beings. In Milton, Satan refuses to admit defeat and corrupts the Garden of Eden through humanity's first act of defiance, the first in a long line of demonic interference in the human world. Indeed, our very fallen nature is itself the direct result of this constant interference of the demonic.

The Fallen Angels themselves have been the focus of many works aimed at identifying, repelling, and even controlling these demonic forces. These include anonymous texts such as The Testament of Solomon, which is perhaps the earliest manual with instructions on how to confront demons. The manual is based on the legend that Solomon enslaved demons to build the First Temple, a decision that ultimately proved mistaken. Later works in the Middle Ages built on this tradition, with Michael Psellus writing On the Operation of Demons in the 11th century, which combined a list of fallen angels as well as ways to cope with their evil influence. Two later publications, the anonymous 15th century The Lanterne of Light and Peter Binsfeld's Treatise on Confessions by Evildoers and Witches from 1589, both identified demonic activity with the Seven Deadly Sins. In both of these systems, each of the Deadly Sins was represented by a powerful demon: Lucifer for Pride, Beelzebub for Envy, Sathanas for Wrath, Abadon for Sloth, Mammon for Greed,

Belphegor for Gluttony, and Asmodeus for Lust. This identification of demonic forces with sin meshes well with the tendency of the possessed to exhibit sinful behaviors. At the same time, church teachings have also suggested that sinful behavior itself may tempt a demon to its host. Other later works in the occult have built on this tradition and drawn up entire systems of demonology intended to do everything from communicating with them to subjugating them to driving them out of their host.[23]

The Cult of Satan and its Manifestations

Followers of Satan have come in many forms. In the earliest accounts from the Old Testament, the cults of Satan and other demons were associated with the pagan gods of nearby tribes such as the Canaanites, the Philistines, and the Babylonians, whose gods were often bloodthirsty and cruel. Gods such as the Canaanite deity Baal, mentioned throughout the Old Testament, would later become one of the principal demons in Satan's army in later Christian tradition. However, the Bible mentions no cults worshiping Satan himself, only groups that

---

[23] Notable examples here include the famous occultist and frequent guest at Rudolph II's notable court Cornelius Agrippa in De occulta philosophia, where he lists "the six authors of all calamities" as Acteus, Megalesius, Ormeus, Lycus, Nicon, and Mimion. *The Lesser Key of Solomon* from the 17th century—probably the most well-known book on the subject—and the *Dictionnaire Infernal* from 1818 are also notable for their combination of a variety of traditions with Catholic demonology.

practiced heathenism or chose to forsake the God of Israel.

By the medieval period, this trend had changed markedly. Certain cults in the Middle Ages came to reason that Satan, not God, was the actual ruler of this earthly realm, giving him the name Rex Mundi, or King of the World. They, in turn, felt that Satan and God's places had been reversed in the Scriptural tradition and chose to worship Satan as God. During the Middle Ages, occultists such as John Dee[24] often dabbled in alchemy, necromancy, and other arts forbidden by the Church, many of which involved the summoning of demonic entities in an attempt to harness their power.

More recent traditions center around the work of Anton LaVey, whose Satanic Bible preaches a creed that privileges the physical over the spiritual and encourages practitioners to embrace this world rather than focus all their energy on the next. At the same time, Satanists in LaVey's tradition are not outright hedonists; instead, they preach a balance between pleasure and pain that is more in line with philosophies like those of Epicurus. Nevertheless, members of the Church of Satan reject the teachings of Christ and embrace the worldliness of Lucifer instead. Their temples feature altars with icons considered blasphemous by the Christian tradition, such as pentagrams, inverted crucifixes, and most prominently, statues and images of Baphomet, a goat-headed incarnation of Satan himself. As a

---

[24] John Dee was a frequent guest at the court of Holy Roman Emperor Rudolph II, an avid occultist who also sponsored the sciences and the arts.

result of these profane practices, members of this cult make themselves vulnerable to demonic attack by forsaking the blessings of the Divine in favor of a path of earthly pleasure.

Other satanic cults are not associated with the Church of Satan and follow much more hideous practices. These include the much-discussed satanic cults of Scandinavia, many of whom are affiliated with death metal bands in the region.[25] These cults made news throughout the 20th century for burning churches throughout Sweden and Norway. They even actively participated in human sacrifice and ritual suicide. According to recent research, this phenomenon is not confined to Scandinavia: "Apparently, well-organized Satanic sects do exist throughout America, and some, at least, are vicious and even homicidal."[26]

In addition to these formally organized groups, Satan gathers followers who may not even be aware they are under his power. Although not technically a cult, those who turn away from God are themselves participating in the rejection of the Divine and embracing materialistic hedonism, a profound threat to spiritual well-being. This tendency seems particularly true today as secularism takes over many corners of the developed world, and faith seems to be fading. Of course, there is no reason we cannot wield both reason and faith in our struggle against evil

---

[25] Ian Christe has an excellent discussion of these cults in his book *The Sound of the Beast.*
[26] Woods, Richard OP. "Satanism Today." In *Soundings in Satanism.* New York: Sheed and Ward, 1972. p. 100

influences in our lives. In fact, in recent decades, the Church has continued to embrace scientific discoveries in combination with the revelations of the Faith. We can therefore live as rational modern citizens without sacrificing the faith that fulfills our spiritual needs.

We should note here, however, that members of satanic cults, whether consciously part of an organized sect or unconsciously upholding satanic practices—are never beyond saving. A perfect example of this hope is Blessed Bartolo Longo (1841-1926), an Italian saint from the 19th century. Beatified by Pope John Paul II (himself now a saint) in 1980, Longo left the Catholic Church after his mother's death and was ordained as a Satanist priest. A participant in seances, orgies, and demonic seances, Longo began struggling with thoughts of suicide over the years. At his darkest moment, the Satanist priest had a vision of the Blessed Virgin Mary, who told him, "If you seek salvation, promulgate the Rosary." Longo renounced Satan on the spot and pledged himself to the Rosary. During a séance after his vision, Longo announced to those present: "I renounce spiritism because it is nothing but a maze of error and falsehood" and went on to be ordained as a Dominican friar in 1871. He would go on to establish a shrine at the site of his vision, the Shrine of Our Lady of Pompeii, which he dedicated to her as the Queen of Victories and Our Lady of the Rosary. The shrine stands today as a monument to the fact that no one, no matter how deeply Satan has them in his grasp, is completely beyond saving, especially through the Virgin Mary's power as an intercessor.[27]

The Action of Satan: Vexation, Possession, Obsession, and Infestation

Satan's interference in our world comes in four general forms: vexation, possession, obsession, and infestation. In his influential work on the topic, An Exorcist Tells His Story (1990), Father Gabriele Amorth—who was for many years the chief exorcist in the Vatican—recounts his own experiences with demonic influence. In the process, he outlines the four general forms and notes his encounters with each. Similar divisions between types of demonic activity have also been noted by practicing exorcists, spiritualists, and mediums from various traditions.

Vexation

Vexation has come in modern times to mean something like "bothering" or "pestering." In matters of spiritual warfare, however, it means something far more serious. Vexation in Scripture means something more like "troubled," "afflicted,"

---

[27] Stagnaro, A. (2016). "Blessed Bartolo Longo, the Ex-Satanist Who Was Freed Through the Rosary." *National Catholic Register*, Dec. 12, 2016.; see also the official website of the Shrine of Our Lady of Pompeii: https://www.ourladyofpompeii.org/welcome/blessed-bartolo-longo-shrine/

or "in anguish" (see Deuteronomy).

Vexations are perhaps the most common type of demonic influence, typically provoked by sinful behaviors, the use of blasphemous spells, or interacting with demons willingly. Unlike possession, cases of vexation do not deprive the afflicted of control over their minds and bodies. Instead, vexations are most often seen as physical and mental attacks on the afflicted, resulting in injuries such as bruises, scratches, or fevers. Often, the vexation victims feel they are being persecuted by the demonic force, constantly fearing the next attack.

Not every vexation is visible. Sometimes vexations take the form of turbulence in personal relationships, unexplainable difficulties at work, or persistent troubles in daily life. Vexations can also take the form of incurable and terrible nightmares or psychological turmoil not directly caused by cognitive problems. Still, the physical manifestations of vexation are the most common signs, evidence that an evil force is at work.

Some well-known examples of vexation come from accounts of the saints. St. Colette of Corbie, the 14th century reformer of the Poor Clares Order, suffered from "diabolic vexations," repeatedly attacked by swarms of insects, reptiles, and even stones. St. Nicholas of Tolentino struggled with demonic beatings throughout his ministry, as did St. Alphonsus Rodriguez, who endured seven years of vexations evident through physical marks and bruises on his body. St. Ignatius of Loyola recounted a series of vexations when he felt as if a demonic force was strangling him. Padre Pio also recounted stories of being whipped by an invisible force, which he identified as vexation from a demonic power.

Possession[28]

Possession is probably the most well-known form of Satanic action. This entails an internal demonic influence, one where the human body is hijacked by an infernal force. In cases of possession, the afflicted literally lose control to the demonic force. In turn, the person loses their individuality, often becoming unidentifiable to their old self. They also often behave violently, curse without hesitation, and exhibit bizarre physical symptoms such as scratches, bruises, or twisted limbs (which are also seen in certain cases of vexation). As exorcist Gabriele Amorth notes in his memoirs, possession remains one of the most startling and incomprehensible examples of the diabolic attempts to influence our human world.

In Mark 5:1-20, we read about perhaps the most intense accounts of possession. The disciples enter the country of the Gadarenes, where they encounter "a man with an unclean spirit, who had his dwelling among the tombs; and no man could bind him, no, not with chains." Mark goes on to describe how the man was wild, often cutting himself with stones, refusing all

[28] Mt 10:8; Mk 3:14-15; 6:13; 16:17; Lk 9:1; 10:17

help. When he sees Jesus, the demoniac begs for Jesus to help him, recognizing him as the Son of God. Jesus then says, "Come out of this man, thou unclean spirit," before asking the spirit's name, to which it replies, "My name is Legion: for we are many." Confronting the evil spirits afflicting the man, Christ casts them into a herd of swine, who are driven into a frenzy by the demons, run to the sea, and drown themselves. Afterwards, the man previously returned to normal, "sitting and clothed and in his right mind." The villagers feared the power of Jesus had demonstrated that he let on his ministry, but the account spread throughout the Levant, and "all men did marvel."

This passage in Mark presents us with several central components of possession and subsequent exorcism. First, the possessed are often considered demented and self-destructive. In this case, none of the afflicted man's fellow citizens attempted to help him, instead casting him out. Second, Jesus treats the man humanely while also recognizing the presence of "unclean spirits" within him. In his act of exorcism, Jesus enacts a decree stating firmly to the demonic entities to leave the man's body. Third, when conversing with the entities directly, Jesus learns they are "Legion," an important reminder that possession is not necessarily limited to a single demonic force.

In Luke 4:33-36, Jesus again encounters a man "which had the spirit of an unclean devil" and casts out the evil force through a forceful invocation of the power of God. In Matthew 4:24, Jesus cures many people of illnesses, including "those which were possessed with devils," and in 12:22, he exorcises a man possessed with a diabolical force that drove him blind and dumb, casting it out and curing him of his afflictions. Later, in Matthew 17:18, Jesus drives the devil out of a young child similarly. The power used by Jesus to cast out demonic presences is noted again in Luke 10:17, where we read that "the seventy returned again with joy, saying, Lord, even devils are subject unto us through thy name." This suggestion of the power of Christ's name alone forms the basis of approaches to possession and exorcism of demonic influence.

Accounts of possession can be found throughout the lives of the saints. St. John of the Cross was renowned for his ability to cast out demonic entities from the possessed, and St. Teresa of Avila was another celebrated exorcist. More recently, exorcisms have received less attention, but as theologian and chief exorcist of Paris, Joseph de Tonquedec notes: "It is true to say that while cases of genuine possession are extremely rare, the patients of whom I speak are innumerable. It would not be legitimate to treat them as possessed, for all the evidence goes to show that they are not. On the other hand, they are not invariably or necessarily mental cases, who would have some chance of a cure through psychology."[29] Tonquedec makes an important point about the transcendent nature of possession, noting that even awareness of psychology cannot explain these tortures.

---

[29] In "Some Aspects of Satan's Activity in This World," p. 40.

Obsession

Obsession concerns when demonic forces outwardly trouble the afflicted instead of the inward affliction of possession. The term was first explored at length by King James himself in his 1597 *Daemonologie*, a noted work of Protestant theology. In it, James notes that demons can interfere with the human world in multiple ways, including spectra, obsession, and possession. Obsession concerns demonic action where the afflicted is subjected to obsessive, often harmful actions. According to Father Amorth, "Obsession occurs when a person is affected by obsessive, invincible thoughts . . . and in extreme cases, suicide." One example of this type of demonic activity can be found in the account of Mary Magdalene di Pazzi, a 16th century Catholic mystic who involuntarily attempted suicide while demonically obsessed. Likewise, St. Anthony the Hermit, St. Catherine of Siena, and St. Gemma Galgani all struggled with demonic obsession—and each is now a powerful intercessor for those facing similar affliction.

Although similar to temptation, obsession is more clearly the work of demonic influence. Unlike vexation or possession, obsession is usually less visible, afflicting the mental and spiritual parts of the person rather than the physical. Still, many of the same techniques are effective at dispelling demonic obsession. Among the most effective are holy water, sacred medals (especially those of the Blessed Mother and St. Benedict), and devotional prayers.

Infestation

Infestation involves demonic activity that does not directly affect a person. Instead, the evidence of demonic activity appears in moving objects, unexplained sounds or voices, smells without an obvious source, and other bizarre happenings that defy the senses. Infestation usually involves a place rather than a person. The most common example of this type of demonic activity comes from accounts of haunted houses or other places. Despite the difference in hosts, the rites of exorcism and related supplications are extremely similar for cases of infestation and possession.

Importantly, we must take care to distinguish demonic infestation from other types of hauntings. In some cases, the signs of infestation such as moving objects, unexplained voices, and strange physical phenomena such as drastic temperature changes result from spirits that are not demonic in nature. These spirits can include ghosts and other phantoms, the transient souls of the deceased unable to move on from this world to the next. These spirits are often tethered to this world due to a tragic death or unfinished business, but they are also often trapped in a state of Limbo. Certain practices used in exorcism, such as invocation and the use of spiritual intercessors, are effective at cleansing spaces of these itinerant spirits as well, but they should not be confused with demons.

Facing Satan: The Exorcism

According to many Biblical scholars, as many as a quarter of the miracles performed by Jesus in the Gospels involved Him casting out demons or confronting Satan directly. Given the sheer number of miracles Christ performed in the New Testament, this may shock even the most seasoned Christian. Throughout Scripture, Jesus instructs his disciples in methods of casting out these demonic entities, primarily by using the sheer force of his name as the Son of God. The Church, as the *de facto* successor of the Apostles and their mission, therefore has a long tradition of practicing exorcisms in the Scriptural manner, although the procedure itself has evolved significantly over the centuries. Each case of exorcism depends on the nature of the possession. In most cases of severe possession, the *Ritual Romanum* is the preferred approach. However, this strategy traditionally requires a Catholic priest, making it less ideal for afflicted people of different faiths.

Unlike sacraments, exorcism is a sacramental, a practice intended to sanctify, though not technically one of the sacraments laid out by Jesus in Scripture. However, exorcism is closely related to The Sacrament of Reconciliation, or Penance, which renews our baptismal vows and restores any grace within us lost through sin. Despite this renewal of our relationship with the divine, there remain instances where the sacrament is not enough to protect the afflicted from diabolic forces. In these instances, exorcism is necessary.

The exorcism process essentially draws directly upon the power of Christ to dispel the presence of Satan and protect the afflicted from future possession. In effect, an official member of the Church serves as the literal representative of Christ and liberates the afflicted from the evil presence. As noted earlier, exorcism accounts occur in Scripture (Mt 17:18 and Luke 4:35, for example). However, there is no explicit ritual given in the Bible except using holy incantations from Psalms, the Prophets, and supplications to God and the Holy Spirit. As it exists today, Exorcism follows this tradition, in conjunction with later additions from the actions of saints and other practitioners. This includes writings by Fathers of the Church such as Athanasius, Cyprian, Tertullian, and Irenaeus, who recount techniques such as invoking Christ's name, using both the sign of the Cross and icons of the Cross itself, exsufflation, and the use of prayers. In many ways, the practice of exorcism is a form of shepherding, where the exorcist leads the evil spirit away from a member of his flock.

Exorcism occurs in two forms: minor and major. Minor exorcisms are performed on adults and children preparing for baptism and on the faithful wishing to be protected from potential demonic influence. The rites for these minor exorcisms can be found in the most recent appendixes to the Rite. The second form, major exorcism, is much more serious and must be administered by a priest, bishop, or higher-level cleric with special approval. According to the *Catechism of the Catholic Church*, major exorcism is intended for "the expulsion of demons or to the liberation ... from demonic possession." Before this ritual is approved, the exorcist must be certain that this is a case of possession, and therefore psychological testing is required before the ritual can proceed. Importantly, the ritual is not restricted to Catholics—or even Christians—but allowed for anyone afflicted who demonstrates a genuine need for liberation from diabolic interference.

Given the strict requirements for approval, major exorcisms are quite rare and become rarer each passing year. Minor exorcisms are more common, given their use to prepare those waiting to be baptized. Any sacramental minister can perform a minor exorcism, and according to "Supplications which May be Used by the Faithful Privately in Their Struggle Against the Powers of Darkness," any clergy person or faithful lay person can perform these rites. On the other hand, the Rite of Major Exorcism is restricted to bishops or specially trained priests. The official text for performing exorcisms is an updated version of the *Rituale Romanum* called *Exorcisms and Related Supplications*. In addition to the readings in the main chapter, the second chapter includes suggestions for supplemental texts while the appendix contains special prayers for especially intense situations of possession or other demonic influence. A last appendix includes various prayers and supplications approved for use by lay faithful, many of which are included in Part 4's arsenal.

The exorcist prayers included in the Rite are the primary

weapon used to drive out the demonic presence. These include Gospel readings, Psalms, and other Scriptural excerpts. The ritual includes more than words, however, involving several symbolic actions that represent the cleansing nature of exorcism. First, holy water is administered to the afflicted, an act designed to recall baptism and the saving power of Christ. Next comes the laying of hands, accompanied by exsufflation, where the exorcist breathes on the afflicted individual's face. The laying of hands recalls Christ laying hands on the sick and possessed throughout the New Testament, while exsufflation is meant to recall the healing power of the Holy Spirit. Lastly, the exorcist performs the presentation of the Cross as they make the sign of the Cross, reminding the evil spirit of Christ's victory over Satan at the time of the Crucifixion.

Two types of formulas are used in the ritual itself: deprecative and imperative. Deprecative formulas are those prayers and supplications to the divine asking for the release of the possessed person from demonic influence. Deprecative formulas serve to call God's attention to the condition of the afflicted and invoke his holiness to bless both the space and those present. Imperative formulas, used in conjunction with deprecative ones, are aimed at the evil presence directly, ordering them to vacate the body of the afflicted. There is a specific order, however, in which the two formulas are used. Deprecative formulas are the most powerful as they invoke God's blessing directly. Therefore, Church law requires deprecative formulas to be used first, followed by imperative ones, if necessary. As a rule, imperative formulas may not be used without deprecative ones.

The site of the ritual is also important, as creating sacred spaces is a crucial part of successful spiritual warfare. First, the site should ideally be one consecrated and isolated from the public, preferably a small chapel or church. Second, although the exorcist alone performs the actual ritual, other faithful or clergy should be present to lend their faith to the force of the exorcist's words and actions.

Decrees

Decrees come in different forms, from the legal to the ecumenical. In matters of spiritual warfare, we can think of decrees as universal truths that embody the eternal Word.

The King James Bible Dictionary defines "decree" as both a legal term for judgment as well as a theological statement regarding the "predetermined purpose of God; the purpose or determination of an immutable Being, whose plan of operations is, like himself, unchangeable." By invoking the eternal divinity of God, we essentially draw his omnipotence within ourselves, creating a powerful weapon against the chaotic forces that seek to undo his Will.

Using decrees against demonic forces effectively brings us

closer to God by embracing his eternal nature and channeling these truths against the lies so commonly whispered by demonic forces. Examples of this occur often in the Scriptures. In Job 22:28, Eliphaz tells Job that so long as he embraces the Lord's mercy, "Thou shalt decree a thing, and it shall be established unto thee, and the light shall shine upon thy ways." By submitting ourselves to divine power, we may, in turn, use decrees to drive out abominations from Creation.

Decrees transform the Word of God—embodied literally in Christ as the Son and Logos—into spiritual action. When we acknowledge ourselves as mouthpieces of the Divine and position our words against evil, we are, in turn, allowing God to speak through us. The Word of God, dictated through holy revelation, provides us with the necessary armaments for our battles against our spiritual enemies. Decrees, therefore, remain one of the strongest forms of language available to us, carrying with them the weight of tradition so repulsive to Satan and his agents. When we invoke decrees in exorcistic rituals, we, in effect, become Christ and thus can better channel our connection to the Father through the intentional force of the Word. This union of words and deeds allows us to bridge the gap between theory and practice and better confront the evil working against us.

PART 3

Practical Steps Toward Victory on the Battlefront

Creating Sacred Space

Creating a sacred space is one of the most important aspects of gaining and maintaining victory. This space is one where demonic forces have little or no power. Above all, we must recognize that all places are potentially sacred, even those that have been defiled in some profane way. Creating such a space can be as simple as blessing it with holy water, mounting a crucifix above the door, or simply filling it with love and laughter, both poisonous to demonic entities.

Although all spaces are sacred, the risk of demonic interference remains in part because evil is not a place but an energy. In belief systems where Hell is the source of evil, we can easily be led to believe that evil is far away and isolated. In fact, evil energy is constantly slithering around our lives. As Milton aptly puts it, after Lucifer is cast out of Heaven, he comments on the nature of Hell itself:

> "Me miserable! Which way shall I fly
>
> Infinite wrath and infinite despair?
>
> Which way I fly is hell; myself am hell;
>
> And in the lowest deep a lower deep,
>
> Still threat'ning to devour me, opens wide,
>
> To which the hell I suffer seems a heaven"

Here, Satan claims that all spaces can be defiled because he, the embodiment of evil, brings that space with him. In order to defend ourselves from this energy, sacred spaces must be created and maintained.

The most obvious sacred spaces are those consecrated by representatives of God Himself. These include churches and cathedrals. These spaces themselves are designed to draw our eyes—and our spirits—up toward Heaven. The monstrance, a special vessel that holds the Eucharist when not in use, is an especially potent source of sacred energy, as is the chalice that holds the Blood of Christ. Yet for us, building a cathedral is not a practical option, so what other methods are available to us?

Statues and icons are traditionally accessible ways to sanctify a space. In Orthodox tradition, icons are perhaps the most noteworthy symbols of holiness, gilded, so they reflect light even at night. Most of these icons depict the Blessed Mother and Infant Jesus, though saints are also shown in many examples. The most notable of these are from the Byzantine Empire, many of which survive in the Hagia Sophia in Istanbul, although it is now a mosque. In the Catholic tradition, statues are a more common method of sanctifying a space. The most popular statuary is the Blessed Mother, which provides powerful protection against evil energy. This defense is made more notable when one considers the Virgin Mary's connection with more ancient fertility goddesses such as Demeter, Ishtar, and Freyja, eternal representations of the Feminine. Other popular statues include the Pietà, which shows Mary cradling the corpse of the recently crucified Jesus. This striking image holds considerable power. Another common figure is the Infant Jesus of Prague, an infant Jesus dressed in imperial robes and a crown meant to symbolize his universal kingdom. All these statues and icons exude positive sacred energy and help sanctify a space.

Candles are another method of sanctification. These can be votary candles dedicated to a given saint or candles blessed for holy purposes. Even though fire is usually associated with the brimstone of Hell, in the case of candles, the fire represents the Holy Spirit and offers protection against negative energy. As a source of light, the candle is a symbol of God's grace as well, which never abandons us no matter how dark the world may become.

Combining several elements into a small altar is perhaps the most effective method of creating a sacred space. Through a mixture of crucifix, votary candles, statues (especially of the Virgin Mother), and icons, a home altar can serve as a barrier against demonic intrusion. A home altar can also function as a site of worship, allowing prayer in a holier space, magnifying the power of the words themselves. When we pray in a sanctified space, each element that contributes to its holiness works in harmony to make the prayer even stronger.

Mindset

Our state of mind directly determines our state of spirit. First and foremost, our minds must be clear of distraction and focused on the task at hand. The best way to achieve this mindset is through meditation via prayer. By directing our attention toward God's grace, we can better elevate our minds above the material world and prepare to engage the spiritual plane. In other words, our mindset must be dedicated to consolation, embracing the light, and armoring ourselves in it.

Furthermore, our minds must be free from sin as much as possible. To achieve this, the sacrament of reconciliation is an excellent method of spiritual cleansing, as by confessing our sins, we are absolved and free to partake in the sacred mysteries of the Eucharist. By participating in the Mass after being absolved, we can fully experience Grace through the Sacrament of Communion, partaking in the Body and Blood of Christ and thereby becoming one with the Divine within us. These sacramental rites, the foundations of the Church's practice, not only bring us into literal communion with God but also purify our spirits and clear our minds of the distraction of sin.

A final technique for establishing the proper mindset is to embrace the positive energy in our life and dispel the negative. If we clad ourselves in the love of our family and friends, our mind becomes more resilient. This love drives away the two most perilous threats to a proper mindset: fear and doubt. With the knowledge that we are not alone, we can cast aside fear. In turn, if we embrace the gift of Christ's sacrifice, we no longer doubt his power. Instead, we recognize there is nothing to fear, not even death itself, because Christ is victorious in all things. His Resurrection showed us that death is but a gateway to a higher existence, one where spirit transcends body into immortal unity with the One. This is the highest form of hope and one that evil cannot abide.

Setting Intentions

Intentionality is more than simply what we mean to do. Instead, intentionality represents our entire being put into action. When using a prayer in spiritual warfare, intentions matter above all else. First, our intention must be both sincere and firm. Without conviction, no amount of prayer can truly drive away an evil intrusive force. Second, our intention must be empowered with belief, our faith imbuing the words with the necessary power they alone cannot project against our enemy. Third, our intention must be clear. We cannot waver in our purpose, whether clearing a defiled space, dispelling a curse, or casting out an unwelcome demonic presence.

Spiritualist Monica Berg addresses intentions in her books Fear is Not an Option and Rethink Love by distinguishing them from goals. The main difference, according to Berg and others, is that "Goals are static and set in the future, and intentions are in the here and now—they're about how you are being in the moment as you work toward your goals." This distinction is extremely important as intentions are a practice of being present rather than a plan for the future, although they are certainly intertwined. Our intentions in a spiritual warfare setting are the immediate needs of ourselves and others in the conflict we are facing.

Setting intentions requires practice. Daily meditation and prayer is one way to accomplish this, especially effective because it quickly becomes a habit. By invoking positive spiritual energy at the outset of each day—and even better, throughout the day—we can better prepare ourselves for times of trouble. Our intentions set through daily prayer include not only a request for divine guidance and protection throughout the day but also reinforcing our faith through practice. Eventually, many of these practices happen almost effortlessly, habits that strengthen us spiritually, mentally, and physically.

Establishing intentions follows a flexible pattern since our intentions can change at any moment in reaction to present conditions. According to experts establishing[30] intention requires several steps. First, we must determine our desired outcome. In general, the more specific this desire, the more powerful our intention. A practical exercise for this step is to write our desire down to get an idea of what we are trying to achieve. Second, we need to establish what qualities we intend to embody. As Berg notes, goals are based on actions while intentions are based on being. To this effect, when establishing intentions, we need to envision who we want to be in the moment, which empowers us to achieve our goals. In cases of spiritual warfare, this includes clearly defining what kind of person we want to be. Saying to ourselves on a given morning, "I am going to be more charitable today," is an example of this practice in action. Third, we need to determine a plan for how to achieve this intention. To continue the above example, if I intend to be more charitable today, then I may outline some acts that will make this possible. I might set a goal of donating to a just cause or helping at a food bank, actions that, in turn, help

---

[30] Including Monica Berg, Amina Al-Tai (a holistic coach working across traditions), and renowned spiritual guru Deepak Chopra.

me realize my intention. Not only does this strengthen me spiritually, but it also takes the abstract virtue of charity and makes it a real positive force of change in the world.

The greatest obstacle to setting intentions is the same that plagues us in almost every spiritual battle: doubt. To effectively establish our intentions, we need to rid ourselves of doubt. The best way to achieve this is to rely on our faith in ourselves and God. One of the means of optimizing this strategy is to practice surrender. As Amina Al-Tai notes, "Surrender isn't waving the white flag or giving up. Surrender is an absence of resistance." This is an especially challenging approach because it requires us to practice humility, one of the Seven Virtues, and sacrifice our Pride. This act is the precise opposite of what Satan wants us to do since he is, above all else, a creature of Pride. Instead of forcing our intentions and attempting to control everything around us, we find ourselves more successful when we submit and surrender to the grace of God. It is no coincidence that Islam means "surrender" or "submission," and this concept is central to the practice of Christianity among the monastic orders in both the Catholic and Orthodox traditions. By surrendering ourselves to God's will, our own wills find their way in the world and enable us to become who we intend to be: soldiers for the Light.

Spiritual Discipline

Too often, we associate discipline with negative outcomes, such as punishment in school or the strict regiments of military training. To prepare ourselves for spiritual warfare, we too must embrace discipline—in all senses of the word. First, we must be willing to put in the hard work as if we were in military training since, in a sense, we are training our spirits for combat. Second, we must be willing to discipline ourselves when we go astray, learning from our mistakes. This last point should remind us that "discipline" comes from the same root word as "disciple," which is what we should strive to become in our spiritual lives. "Disciple" itself comes from the Latin dis-cere, which means "to learn." In this sense, to practice discipline is to become a disciple of Light and participate in a constant practice of learning.

There are several approaches to how exactly one should approach spiritual discipline. In his Discipline of the Spirit (1963), Howard Thurman—civil rights activist, poet, minister, philosopher—outlined five principles of spiritual discipline: commitment, growth in wisdom and stature, suffering, prayer, and reconciliation. The first principle, commitment, includes both commitment to God through following Scripture as well as commitment to one's family, one's community, and one's values. The second principle, growth in wisdom and stature, involves both intellectual growth through lifelong education and personal growth, as personal faith nurtures success. The third principle, suffering, is perhaps one of the most important. Thurman does not necessarily mean we should intentionally suffer. Instead, he means that we need to recognize that suffering makes us stronger and brings us closer to God through Christ. After all, the Crucifixion, in many ways, represents the ultimate suffering, but one that led to salvation through sacrifice. Many Catholic saints—especially St. Francis of Assisi, St. Ignatius of Loyola, and Mother Theresa—placed suffering among the greatest human experiences because it brings us in tune with the human condition and nurtures compassion within our spirits. The fourth principle, prayer, is one constant among all approaches to spiritual discipline. Whether through meditation, spiritual readings, or the Scripture, prayer brings our spirit in line with the divine. Lastly, reconciliation is the final principle in Thurman's system. This principle operates in two ways: reconciling ourselves with God and reconciling ourselves with others. The first requires us to give ourselves over to His grace, the second requires us to forgive without hesitation. Forgiveness not only brings us closer to a Christ-like life but also strengthens our spirit with the power of Mercy.

Other approaches to spiritual discipline follow a similar path, but some additional practical suggestions give us more tools. If we think of the spirit as a sword intended to protect us from evil, these suggestions are whetstones to keep that sword sharp. An excellent practical guide for daily spiritual discipline comes from Pope Benedict, who patterned his discipline after his predecessor, Pope John Paul II.[31] The first thing both pontiffs recommend is beginning every day with 30 minutes of mental

---

[31] George Weigel's book, *Witness to Hope*, Chapter 9, "Be Not Afraid!" presents an excellent version of PJP II's daily rituals.

prayer. This form of meditation doesn't necessarily have to be reciting prayer, but instead simply quieting the mind, listening to God, and reestablishing your personal relationship with the Divine. Benedict also recommends attending Mass daily, although this may be difficult given modern schedules. In lieu of Mass, he recommends an hour of verbal prayer at some point in the day. Praying the Rosary daily is another important element of this spiritual discipline, a practice Pope John Paul II suggested performing in front of an image of the Blessed Mother. Other suggested prayers include the Angelus and the Regina Coeli, three times daily at morning, noon, and night in the monastic tradition.

In addition to prayer, effective spiritual discipline requires reading. These could be Scriptural or spiritual classics such as The Imitation of Christ by Thomas a Kempis, Introduction to the Devout Life by St. Francis de Sales, or the lives of the saints. The regimen suggests doing these readings at night when you have time to reflect on your day. This spiritual reading can go beyond the classics, of course. Any kind of reading can be a form of meditation that allows us to expand our understanding of the infinite, both within us and within the world around us.

These various approaches to spiritual discipline are suggestions but include techniques for growing as a spiritual being. By reading the works of the saints and other great spiritual thinkers, we ourselves gain part of their wisdom, experiencing the type of growth Thurman recommends. Praying throughout the day means we never lose sight of our connection to the Divine. This alone protects us from the influence of demonic forces in our life because we remain vigilant. By establishing a personal relationship with God, especially through Christ and the Blessed Mother, we participate in the sacred mysteries of the universe. In other words, we become disciples through discipline because we never stop learning to deepen our connection to the Light. As a result, discipline arms us for confrontations with Satan, who may at any moment enter our lives and attempt to sow chaos.

Strengthening Yourself Against Spiritual Attack

To strengthen ourselves against spiritual attack, we must go beyond mere discipline. We must go beyond establishing sacred space, proper mindset, even intentions. To truly strengthen ourselves against spiritual attack, we must arm ourselves with the proper weapons. Many of these weapons will be discussed in detail within Part 5 on maintaining victory, but in spiritual warfare, as in all forms of competition, defense is crucial. As King David reminds us, "The Lord is my rock, my fortress and my deliverer; my God is my rock, in whom I take refuge, my shield and the horn of my salvation. He is my stronghold, my refuge and my savior" (2 Samuel 22:2-3). We can think of strengthening ourselves spiritually in the same way as we think of physical training. First, we need a regimen, one that we ideally practice daily. Second, we need to focus on building up our spiritual resources through faith and determination to live as positively as possible. Third, we need those sacred tools— sacramentals, blessed objects, the Word itself—which provide additional protection against all forms of satanic influence.

Daily prayer or meditation is the first step because it provides a basic shield against attack. Although no single prayer covers all circumstances, some general orisons such as The Prayer to St. Gabriel, The Prayer for Strength, and various invocations of saints and angels are effective. These benedictions are specifically designed to fortify our faith by affirming our belief in God and his Word. From the Archangels, we draw the holy strength of Heaven's armies, the very same armies that cast Satan from Heaven. From the saints, we draw the piety and wisdom that comes from knowing that God is with us always and will never abandon us. From our understanding of Christ's sacrifice and the love of his Blessed Mother, we draw the power of the New Covenant that washes away not only the sins within all of us but also the sins of humanity across all time. When we pray using the words of the Tradition, we draw on a truly cosmic spiritual force, aligning ourselves with the Creator against that terrible adversary, Satan.

Another useful tool in this struggle is ritual fasting. This practice has a long history in the Tradition, especially among ascetic practitioners in the monastic orders who have long believed that depriving the body in combination with prayer strengthens the spirit exponentially. Although fasting is an integral part of practice during sacred periods such as Lent and Advent, fasting also provides a means of strengthening the spirit through sacrifices of the body. Of course, fasting must be carefully managed—it's not, after all, simply starvation. Instead, fasting echoes Christ's practice in the desert, where he fasted for forty days and nights to purify himself for his encounter with Satan. As a ritual of purification, it also recalls Paul's injunction in his First Letter to the Corinthians: "For we are the temple of the living God...let us purify ourselves from everything that contaminates body and spirit, perfecting holiness out of reverence for God" (6:16-7:1).

Although usually associated with holy seasons such as Lent or Advent, fasting can be practiced any time of the year as an excellent means of boosting our spiritual stamina. Furthermore, fasting doesn't have to be restricted to food alone. When we deprive ourselves of anything that usually gives us pleasure—going to events, playing games, doing hobbies—we are still making an intentional sacrifice, giving up a pleasurable activity in exchange for the gift of grace.

Other means of strengthening ourselves appear at first like acts of weakness. The most effective of these means is the practice of humility. As the Demon of Pride, Lucifer finds humility most repugnant of all virtues, being as it is the opposite of Pride. In her mystical writings, Teresa found that humility was one of the best means of fortifying herself against attack. "For my own part," she writes in The Foundations, "I believe that His Majesty will not allow him [the devil], or give him power, to deceive anyone with such appearances unless the person himself is to blame...I mean that for humble souls no deception is possible."[32] Teresa's words give us both a means of reinforcing ourselves against attack and a potent weapon against demonic forces.

Weapons and Strategies

Our arsenal contains many weapons for use against darker interferences. As St. Paul the Apostle reminds us, "For though we live in the world, we do not wage war as the world does. The weapons we fight with are not the weapons of the world. On the contrary, they have divine power to demolish strongholds" (2 Cor. 10:2-4). First and foremost, our most powerful weapons are words. As noted at the beginning of John's Gospel, "In the beginning was the Word, and the Word was with God, and the Word was God." Nothing wields more power than words, but the Word itself trumps all others in sheer might. As we saw in the Rite of Major Exorcism, readings from Scripture make up the most potent source of power we have against satanic influence. We can think of this as God speaking through us, and every time we recite Scripture, we act as a mouthpiece for the

---

[32] *Foundations*, p. 41.

Divine.

The use of sacred words appears in the Gospel during one of the more famous encounters between Christ and demons. As we discussed in our investigation of exorcism in the Gospel of Mark, Jesus cast spirits from the demoniac in Gadarene into swine. Indeed, the practice of transference, forcing the possessing force from one being (human) into another (animal), has a long tradition across cultures. One thing to note in this case, though, is that transference is yet another tool at our disposal. With the proper intention combined with the correct words and rituals, we can force a demonic presence from a person or place into another in the same way that Christ did with the possessed man. However, we should note here that this rarely works with other non-living things or inanimate objects. That is, Jesus cast the legion of demons out from the man into swine, not into a bottle or a tree. This suggests that sentience seems to be a necessary property of the host for the parasitic nature of the demon, swine, in particular, sharing remarkable anatomical parallels with humans.[33] The point here is that transference is possible, but we must always consider what kind of host we are dealing with in these situations.

Although we have already discussed many tools for protection, beyond the Rite of Major Exorcism, except for the above-mentioned transference, we haven't seen many offensive

---

[33] Swine are also "unclean" in Jewish tradition, which is part of the reason why they were acceptable hosts in Jesus's exorcism. Paradoxically, in Chinese and Celtic traditions, the sow represents fertility and good fortune.

techniques. One of the most important is what theologian Elizabeth McAlister calls "aggressive prayer." McAlister defines this type of prayer as "any prayer—to the monotheistic god of the orthodox monotheistic traditions or to any other deity or spirit—that seeks to harm, debilitate, move, remove, or change another party."[34] McAlister makes a valid point when she states that most people think of prayer as a submissive act rooted in devotion, love, and peace. However, she found that prayer can also be weaponized throughout history and across cultures. She first noticed this approach among American Evangelicals, whom she saw actively praying for harm against political opponents such as abortion providers and even then-President Obama. This type of prayer shares many of the features of curses. In fact, McAlister notes that this form of prayer is increasingly common in African Pentecostalism, which shares roots with Afro-Haitian practices. In this tradition, aggressive prayer is a form of justice, targeting parties the aggrieved see as unjust.

McAlister notes that "spiritual warfare prayer" is "the most explicit kind of aggressive prayer in the Protestant world . . . bound up in a very complicated theory of justice." This theory of justice relates to the Fall and the fact that, despite Satan tempting Eve, she ate the forbidden fruit of her own free will. As a result, spiritual warriors feel they must fight Satan's influence wherever they find it, by whatever means necessary,

---

[34] From Reverberations: New Directions in the Study of Prayer, "Prayer in Wider Perspective: Spiritual Warfare and Aggressive Prayers" (2015)

to bring about the fulfillment of Christ's sacrifice and truly redeem the world through absolute global conversion. Although this approach is extreme, the principle behind the strength of aggressive prayer remains.

The primary challenge remains maintaining a balance between militarizing prayer and directing it toward the proper targets. For our purposes, those targets are demonic influences in the world that interfere with spiritual well-being. The risk of following the errors of the Crusades or early Islam—where prayer was quite literally a weapon that ultimately devastated communities and led to massacres—poses an obstacle for anyone wishing to practice spiritual warfare without committing these same mistakes. Similarly, the Jesuits were for a time extremely militant in their approach, especially in their aggressive missions in South America, but have dialed down that aggression to focus on more humane approaches to faith.

These warnings are important to keep in mind because one of the things we've established thus far is what does and does not count as demonic interference. In many American Evangelical circles, for example, the Statue of Liberty is considered demonic because it represents the Roman goddess Libertas; there is even an active petition to have it torn down. This extreme interpretation of the demonic is precisely why identifying demonic influence is such an important first step in conducting genuine spiritual warfare based on spiritual observation and discernment rather than in political mumbo-jumbo.

The prayers in our arsenal follow a certain set of standards, coming from a long-standing tradition with proven results across situations. Although they are in English, the prayers are effective in any language, as the Catholic Church acknowledges itself as the "one truly catholic and apostolic church." The term "catholic" itself comes from the Latin for "universal," a pronouncement that the Church upholds the true teachings and practices of Christ and his disciples. After all, the first Pope was none other than St. Peter, the first Apostle, and therefore a direct line of tradition springs from Christ to the contemporary Church. Although many practices have evolved over time, the fundamental mission of the Church remains eternal: to spread Christ's teachings to bring redemption to the people of the world and cast out all of Satan's influence from it.

Conducting a Spiritual Warfare Interview

A spiritual warfare interview can take several forms depending on the nature of the demonic activity involved, whether obsession, vexation, infestation, or possession. What is the purpose of such an interview? For one, it helps us determine which type of demonic interference we're dealing with to adjust our strategy appropriately. For another, it allows us to identify the type of interference we are encountering, from minor demons to the principalities of Hell. A spiritual warfare interview can also determine whether a deliverance prayer session is a better option than a more involved ritual such as exorcism.

In less severe cases of demonic interference, the spiritual warfare interview consists of questions focusing on the problem facing the afflicted person. Have they had encounters with demonic presences in the past? Do they have a family history of spiritual disturbances or mental illness? Are they facing external anxieties that non-supernatural causes could explain? How would they describe their current spiritual state and their relationship with their faith? All these questions aim to determine the core problem at hand, allowing us to explore options to solve it.

In more severe cases, such as possession, such an interview may not be possible as described, given that the afflicted person is under the control of a demonic presence. Even if answers were given, they couldn't be trusted, given the demonic tendency toward lying and manipulation. The demon may be telling us what we want to hear, or they may be outright fabricating to confuse us. In these cases, the interview needs to be adjusted to account for the tricks common to demonic entities. One important note to consider is that anyone attempting to engage the possessing spirit should not speak to it directly, nor allow it to draw any information. Even something as simple as a name can hold great power, and demons will use any opportunity to take advantage of those present. As Adam Christian Blai notes in his discussions of exorcism, attempting to address the demon directly can, in turn, lead to greater devastation, giving the demon influence over not just the afflicted but also others in the vicinity.

Ideally, a spiritual warfare interview involves a clergy member, a *peritus* approved by the Vatican to advise in the process, a medical professional in the event of a physical injury, and members of the faithful, preferably those with experience involving demonic entities. Of course, assembling a roster with all these members is not easy, so alternative arrangements are possible. At the very least, there must be three faithful in the room with the afflicted to conduct the interview at this level. The presiding counselor or clergyman must then begin asking questions as outlined in the *Rituale Romanum* to determine the number of spirits involved and their status in the demonic hierarchy. As we recall from our discussion of Jesus' exorcism in Gadarene, many possession cases involve multiple spirits, "for they are legion." Once the specifics are determined, then the proper strategy can be established.

Determining this strategy again relies on the type of demonic interference, the number of entities involved, the status of these entities, and the condition of the afflicted. Special care must be taken with afflicted individuals in extremely weakened states since the risk of bodily harm or even death is always possible in these cases. Therefore, the spiritual warfare interview is a precursor to the Rite of Major Exorcism, and indeed to any form of demonic interference requiring a spiritual intervention.

Conducting a deliverance session

Where do we turn when our crises are not as severe as vexation, obsession, infestation, or possession? What if we are facing fallout from a curse, mishaps with occult practices, or misfortunes that may or may not be demonic? What if our life problems are partially but not entirely spiritual in nature? That is the role of a deliverance prayer session. A deliverance prayer session[35] is a gathering of faithful intended to help an individual in crisis when no other form of intervention seems to be helping. The purpose of such sessions is to welcome Christ into the session space and through his grace resolve these issues through spiritual means.

There are many instances when a deliverance prayer session is the best option. These include: cases of severe depression and anxiety that therapy and medicine have failed to treat, struggles with forgiveness, repeated battles with temptation or sin, relationship troubles, unspecified negative influence or curses, and negative residual energy from improper dealings with the occult.[36] In all these cases, the problem is spiritual but not

---

[35] A ministry known as The Catholic Centurion is one example of an operation providing such sessions at the clerical and lay level:
https://www.catholiccenturion.com/prayer-sessions-catholic-deliverance-ministry
[36] As we've mentioned, the strict interpretation of "occult" followed by many Christian denominations includes many different practices that are otherwise harmless, and sometimes even beneficial. Most of these practices are banned based on Old Testament law in Deuteronomy and Leviticus, including any form of prognostication (astrology, horoscopes, palmistry, tarot, etc.) which is forbidden. However, these rules are often taken to extremes in the case of many fundamentalist Christian sects, some of which go so far as to claim that weather reporters are sinners because they are practicing a form of predicting the future. This is, of course, an exaggerated interpretation of the moratorium on the occult in

necessarily demonic, although there may be demonic forces at work. One of the primary benefits of deliverance prayer sessions is that they bring the person in crisis into contact with others willing to help. Too often people facing spiritual crises face these challenges alone, feeling too embarrassed to ask for help or too defeated to even try. With the spiritual support of others bringing their positive energy to the session, these interventions can produce wonderful results.

The process of conducting a deliverance prayer session is quite different from that of an exorcism, though it shares many similarities with spiritual warfare interviews. First and foremost, the individual in crisis—in this case usually referred to as "the client" among professional deliverance session providers— finds themselves in need of assistance. Usually, the individual is the party that reaches out for aid, but sometimes they are encouraged by friends and family or perhaps even enrolled for a session by one of these concerned parties. This first step is the most important one, much like the First Step in Alcoholics Anonymous, which requires that the drinker admit they have a problem and submit themselves to a higher power. In fact, this step is critical in almost all recovery programs, whether the vice is drinking, gambling, sex, narcotics, video games, or any other compulsive behavior that runs out of control. This similarity is because deliverance prayer sessions are based on a medical model much like these other programs, a model that remains

---

the Bible, which more accurately forbids practices that rely on any power other than God or his agents (angels, saints, etc.).

one of the most successful formulas for treating all sorts of problems.

The second step involves an interview with the counselor, a role we can take on ourselves after sufficient experience in spiritual warfare. When conducting the interview, we must remember that this second step is primarily about compiling the necessary information about the client: what type of problem they are facing, what steps, if any, they've already taken to address it, and any other issues they might be struggling with which might interact with their spiritual one. Another series of questions involve family history: does your family have any past encounters with these problems? Have you or your family previously struggled with demonic interferences such as obsession, vexation, infestation, or possession? Are you aware of any generational curses that might still be afflicting you or your family? Perhaps most importantly, how would you describe your current spiritual condition? Are you alienated from the Church or still practicing the faith? If you've lost faith in God, have you lost it entirely (as in cases of atheism or extreme agnosticism), or are you simply experiencing intense doubt? When did you last go to confession? All these questions are relevant in a deliverance prayer session interview.

After the interview, we as counselors need to consider the problem at hand. If we feel the issue is better treated by psychiatric professionals, therapists, or experts in another field, then we need to be honest with both ourselves and our client and tell them so. This step can be difficult because it can require tough truths. Many people, especially in religious communities, are often skeptical of medical practices in psychology and psychiatry, especially in rural areas.[37] Nevertheless, if we feel that the client is facing an issue that is not spiritual, we should refer them to the appropriate professionals. At the same time, we must respect their privacy and dignity, so consent is necessary in all cases. As we run through possible diagnoses of the problem, we need to use deductive reasoning to eliminate all unlikely causes until reaching the most likely set of underlying forces. This is the same procedure used by physicians when diagnosing a patient.

Once we have determined the nature of the crisis, we must ensure the client is fully aware of our findings. Openness and honesty are key in these interactions because we are trying to build trust with clients so they can make informed decisions. Again, the deliverance prayer session is just like the patient-centered model in medicine: they have the final say. If they agree about the diagnosis, the next step is proposing a spiritual treatment plan. These plans can vary greatly in length and complexity depending on the nature of the problem. Some crises might be resolved after a single deliverance prayer session; others might take months or even years to handle.

The most common approaches for spiritual treatment are

---

[37] This trend is especially prominent in the United States but occurs around the world.

similar to the purification rituals that are part of Catholic practice and strategies from spiritual warfare. First, all clients are encouraged to take up a daily prayer regimen, which is necessary for strengthening the spirit and reestablishing any lost connections with the Divine. This prayer regimen varies from client to client, but several prayers are fundamental, including the *Our Father*, the *Hail Mary*, the *Apostle's Creed*, and invocations of the saints and angels. Also, many deliverance prayer session organizers highly recommend reciting spiritual warfare prayers, such as those provided later in Part 4. These prayers are powerful benedictions capable of dispelling negative energies and have a proven track record of resolving great and small spiritual crises. This part of the deliverance program is both the easiest and most difficult for several reasons.

On the one hand, praying while in crisis can be a challenge since the client is preoccupied with other concerns. They are also likely praying alone, so it is difficult for us to determine for certain if they are keeping up with their prayer program. On the other hand, praying is the simplest act available to us to bring us into closer proximity to God's grace—even a child can pray and receive God's blessing.

The second part of the program involves getting involved in the Church again by participating in the Mass. The Mass is not just a weekly duty but a way to open our hearts to God's voice. Through the Liturgy, the client will be exposed once again to the Word of God, itself a powerful agent of healing. When the priest delivers the Mass, he is acting *in persona Christi*, literally "in the person of Christ." This is an important concept in the faith because when the priest administers Mass—and especially during the Sacrament of Holy Communion—the priest literally acts in Christ's place. So, when we hear the Liturgy during Mass, we hear the Words of God recited as if hearing them from the mouth of Jesus himself. Similarly, when we receive the Eucharist from the priest, we receive it from Christ as if we were an Apostle at the Last Supper. This alone is a forceful positive experience.

The third part of the program follows from the second: the client must again participate in the Sacraments. Of course, not all seven sacraments are required here, with Baptism, Confirmation, Matrimony, Holy Orders, and Last Rites all singular sacraments. Instead, the client must participate in the Sacraments of Reconciliation and Holy Communion. In Reconciliation, the act of confession is an effective way of purifying the spirit, ridding the confessor of sins, and restoring them to the state of Grace granted by Baptism. Subsequently, when the priest recommends the appropriate acts of penance, the client can redeem themselves through both words and deeds, practical ways to build up the person after facing so much defeat during their crisis. With this purification of spirit, the client is also now permitted to accept the Eucharist, both the Body and Blood of Christ, the central Sacrament in the faith. When the priest transubstantiates the host and wine into the Body and Blood, those who receive the Sacrament are participating in the great mystery of the faith and affirming their dedication to Christ and his teachings.

The last part of the program involves targeted practices. This includes deliverance sessions, which are central to the final victory. Deliverance sessions involve a group of faithful and potentially clergy who gather around the individual in crisis and pray over them, often accompanied by a laying of hands. Specifically, designed deliverance prayers, which we will turn to in Part 4, aim to drive out the negative influence in the afflicted person's life and restore their place in the Light of God. During the session, the afflicted person is anointed with either holy water or chrism (or both), then blessed with a deliverance prayer. The deliverance group then proceeds to take turns reading from Scripture, devotional books, and other materials from the Catechism. In more recent years, letters from friends and family are sometimes read in conjunction with these prayers, a technique often used in Kairos retreats. This demonstrates to the afflicted person that they are not alone and are loved by those closest to them as well as by God Himself.

During these sessions, either the afflicted or one of the counselors will recite an intercessory, asking God for guidance and love. Oftentimes, these intercessions will relieve the afflicted person and bring tremendous comfort. In cases where this does not solve the issue, the afflicted may have a revelation and ask to seek help from another source. Although this might seem like a contradiction given the first steps of the interview itself, it is actually a fulfillment of the deliverance session's promise: answers from the Source. In cases where the client chooses another method of help, that decision itself is an answer to those very same prayers for guidance.

One final step to consider is that if the individual in crisis is facing a curse brought on by an occult object, then that object must be destroyed. How best to destroy the object varies from case to case, but one method applies to all objects: burning. This same method is recommended for disposing of unusable blessed objects,[38] but in the case of occult objects, fire is also preferred. Burning the object destroys the physical object and disperses any residual negative energies from curses or other spells. Destroying the object is a critical part of the deliverance session if the root cause of the crisis in question is, in fact, some type of curse.

Help From The Saints

What if the human assistance provided by deliverance prayer sessions and other interventions is not enough? To whom should we turn if we feel we need additional soldiers in our battle against spiritual darkness? One of the most powerful weapons at our disposal is the assistance of saints. Many of these saints are those who during their earthly lives fended off attacks

---

[38] As noted by the Diocese of Superior in their excellent guide on disposing of blessed religious items with dignity.

from diabolical forces. St. Catherine of Siena (1347-80) famously performed an exorcism to cast a demonic force from a possessed woman in medieval Italy. The scene was memorialized by the Renaissance painter Fungai and showed St. Catherine beseeching the power of God and his Host to drive out the evil spirit. St. Catherine is also the patron saint of protection from fire due to an incident as a girl when she was miraculously spared from a fire, a protection which her biography explains as "the fire of holiness in her heart kept at bay the heat of the flames."[39] This protection from fire extends to hellfire, the element of the demonic. For this reason, St. Catherine remains one of the more powerful intercessors for saintly protection.

St. Joseph, the foster-father of Jesus and patron of the Universal Church, presents one of the strongest intercessors. As head of the Holy Family, he served as the earthly guardian of Jesus throughout his childhood. Yet his title as St. Joseph the "Terror of Demons" positions him to help us in times of crisis.[40] As Paul Thigpen notes, "this title suggests that when we call on him for rescue from our diabolical adversaries, he need not even speak to them: His very presence terrifies them and sends them fleeing."[41] This tradition goes back to Pope Pius XI, who invoked St. Joseph against the demonic effects of Soviet

---

[39] Hallam 1994, p. 158)
[40] Joseph's role in exhortations is covered in great depth by Pope St. John Paul II in *Redemptoris Custos: On the Person and Mission of St. Joseph in the Life of Christ and of the Church.*
[41] From Thigpen's interview with *Angelus News*, https://angelusnews.com/voices/spiritual-warfare-and-the-saints-who-help/

communism, the first instance of St. Joseph being widely invoked as "Terror of Demons." Another example of St. Joseph's power over the demonic comes to us from St. Faustina, one of the most important saints in matters of spiritual warfare. As she wrote after her encounter with Christ, "St. Joseph urged me to have constant devotion to him…He has promised me this special help and protection."[42]

Other saints such as Padre Pio have repeatedly asserted the power St. Joseph wields over demons, claiming that in times of spiritual crisis, we should all "go to Joseph with extreme confidence, because I do not remember having asked anything from St. Joseph without having obtained it readily." More recently, Father Donald Calloway, a contemporary practitioner of spiritual warfare, discusses Joseph's role as Terror of Demons in his *Consecration to St. Joseph*. As he notes, Scripture has little to say about Joseph's anti-demonic abilities, but the various accounts of exorcisms frequently agree that "invoking the name of St. Joseph has brought frantic responses from the demon in the afflicted person." Indeed, Joseph instills fear in demons in large part because his piety during Christ's life protected the child who would become the bane of all evil. Calloway takes this further when he states, "After the Virgin Mary, demons fear St. Joseph more than any other saint." As the protector of Christ the Child, Joseph is also our protector

---

[42] In Faustina's diary, passage 1203.

against the workings of Satan.[43]

Another group of powerful saints are the angels themselves, specifically St. Michael, St. Raphael, St. Gabriel, and St. Uriel. These archangels possess significant powers against evil and can act as mighty intercessors in the face of demonic attack. Mentioned in the New Testament in both the Epistle of St. Jude (9) and St. Paul's First Letter to the Thessalonians (4:15), archangels operate as the order of angels most involved in our lives. Their proximity to the human world makes them especially helpful in spiritual warfare. As we read in Psalms (91:11-12), "For He shall give His angels charge over thee, to keep thee in all thy ways. They shall bear thee up in their hands." They remain at the vanguard of God's armies and lend us their heavenly strength in times of spiritual crisis as among the closest spirits to the Lord.

St. Michael, in particular, is a favorite source of grace, given both his closeness to God and his role in casting Satan and his minions into the Underworld. Much of this tradition comes from the writings of St. Thomas Aquinas, often called the Angelic Doctor, who wrote extensively about the intercessory power of angels in moments of crisis. As the nemesis of Satan in his war against Heaven, St. Michael empowers us as soldiers in the Church militant, a role fundamental to orders such as the

---

[43] Blessed Bartolo Longo, a former satanic priest before his conversion, said: "It is a great blessing for souls to be under the protection of the saint [Joseph] whose name makes demons tremble and flee."

Jesuits.

St. Gabriel serves as another powerful saintly archangel capable of interceding on our behalf. Gabriel appears throughout Scripture as a protector of mankind. In tradition based on Genesis, Gabriel is the Governor of Eden and the overseer of humankind. In the Book of Daniel, the archangel interprets the prophet's visions and announces the coming of the Messiah, a prophecy fulfilled by the coming of Christ. As the archangel charged with announcing to Mary that she would bear the Son of God, Gabriel provides us with a close connection to the Sacred Mysteries of both the Annunciation and the Incarnation. In the Gospel of Luke, Gabriel also announces the birth of St. John the Baptist to his father Zacharias. As the Herald of God, Gabriel is also a crucial part of God's presence on earth and a critical player in the Apocalypse. Depicted with a spear, shield, and scepter, Gabriel is, like Michael, a warrior of God through whom we can summon strength in our own battles.

St. Raphael is much less known than his two fellow archangels. His only appearance in Scripture comes from the Apocrypha,[44] when in the Book of Tobias, he appears disguised as a man calling himself Azarias and joins Tobias on his travels. During

---

[44] As a reminder, the Apocrypha refer to twelve books not recognized by orthodox Judaism or by most Protestant denominations, but which are included in the Septuagint, the Latin Vulgate of St. Jerome, and the contemporary Catholic canon. They include: Esdras (the Book of Ezra and the Book of Nehemiah), Tobit (the Book of Tobias), Judith, Esther, Wisdom of Solomon, Sirach (Ecclesiasticus of Jeremiah), Baruch (with the Epistle of Jeremy), the Song of the Three Holy Children (part of the Book of Daniel 3), the History of Susanna (Daniel 13), Bel and the Dragon (Daniel 14), the Prayer of Manasseh (omitted in deuterocanonical edition), and the Book of Maccabees (1 Maccabees and 2 Maccabees).

their journey, Raphael protects Tobias, in particular when he binds a demon who had killed a woman's seven husbands. Years later, the archangel heals Tobias of blindness, revealing himself as "the angel Raphael, one of the seven, who stand before the Lord" (Tobit 12:15). The seven to whom Raphael refers are the same as the seven archangels who appear in Revelation (8:2), although they remain unnamed in that Scripture. In fact, throughout the entire Biblical canon, the only named archangels are Michael, Gabriel, and Raphael.[45] Raphael's status as both a healer and a binder of demons places him high in the order of angels and saints, especially when we consider his identification with the "angel of the Lord" described in the Gospel of John (5:1-4) where "an angel of the Lord descended at certain times into the pond; and the water was moved. And he that went down first into the pond after the motion of the water was made whole of whatsoever infirmity he lay under." Raphael's healing powers, both physical and spiritual, are thus helpful in our own struggles against demonic infirmities and interferences, especially when the entity needs to be bound, as Raphael did with Tobias.

Yet no more powerful saintly intercessor exists than the Blessed Virgin Mary. In account after account from medieval Catholic mystics, it is only through the power of the Blessed Mother that demonic influence can truly be expelled. In the 13th century,

[45] Other archangels are mentioned in the Book of Enoch, which is not included in the canon but remains relevant as part of the many apocryphal texts that have come down both through tradition and through recent archaeological discoveries (i.e., The Dead Sea Scrolls, the Nag Hammadi Scriptures, Gnostic texts, etc.). In Enoch, other archangels listed are Uriel, Sariel, Raguel, and Jerahmeel.

Blessed Egidius of Portugal—an occultist before his later conversion to the clergy—allegedly made a pact with the devil. This pact led to seven years of torment until beseeching the Blessed Mother, the pact was broken, and Egidius was freed from his affliction and forgiven. Similarly, in the 16th century, St. Juan del Castillo resolved his possession through a combination of prayer and icons of the Virgin Mary. Throughout ecclesiastical history, we see saints and laypeople seek assistance from the Mother of God, who, as Queen of Heaven, wields a power beyond any other spirit besides the Trinity in the Catholic tradition.

Other saints wield special power against demonic forces. St. Benedict, St. Gemma Galgani, and St. Anthony the Hermit remain among the most effective saints to invoke in instances of such encounters with evil. St. Genevieve (ca. AD 420-500), the patron saint of disasters, is another useful intercessor. As one of the Christians responsible for converting Clovis, King of the Franks, Genevieve holds an important place in the history of the Church militant. She is also associated with several confrontations against demons, the most notable of which was depicted in a 13th century illuminated manuscript. The image shows Genevieve confronting a demonic entity equipped with a Bible, a sword (the Sword of Christ), and a censor with an angelic guardian behind her reinforcing her spirit.[46] Another

---

[46] The manuscript is kept at the Censier de l'Abbaye Sainte-Genevieve in France, catalogued as Ms 16261 fol.13v St. Genevieve fighting a demon with the help of an angel, from the Censier de lAbbaye Sainte-Genevieve (Frau 16261 fol.13v St. Genevieve bekämpft einen Dämon mit Hilfe eines Engels, von der Censier de l'Abbaye Sainte-Genevieve)

saint often invoked on both sides of the Atlantic is St. Patrick, whose "breastplate" is a prayer sometimes recited for protection against evil interference. In England, St. George is often invoked in his role as a soldier and a dragonslayer, the dragon being one of Satan's many traditional forms.

Certain saints also lend us extra support against specific temptations. When we are tempted to anger (or more perilously, the Deadly Sin of Wrath), for example, a prayer to St. Jerome can help us, given the saint's personal struggles with rage. Ranked as one of the Four Great Doctors of the Church, St. Jerome was also known for being "short-tempered and cantankerous" and notoriously easy to anger.[47] When we are struggling with temptations toward Lust, a prayer to St. Benedict increases our defenses because the saint—a 6th century monk whose "Holy Rule" formed the basis of all monastic discipline—was an avid promoter of chastity, the capital virtue opposite Lust. As Paul Thigpen recounts, Benedict himself faced a demonic vexation of lust but dispelled the temptation by praying and throwing himself into a thornbush in an act of mortification.[48] Other temptations also vulnerable to certain saints include pride (St. Ignatius of Loyola), despair (St. Padre Pio), and discouragement (St. Teresa of Avila).

In addition to these saintly intercessors, the power of a saint against evil is magnified on their given feast day, another

[47] (Hallam 54).
[48] Thigpen. P. (2016). *Saints Who Battled Satan: Seventeen Holy Warriors Who Can Teach You How to Fight the Good Fight and Vanquish Your Ancient Enemy.*

weapon in our arsenal. The more popular Feast Days have largely been absorbed by Western culture at large—namely the Feast of St. Patrick (March 17th), the Feast of St. Valentine (February 14th), and the Feast of St. Joseph (May 1st)—but by keeping our spirits focused on the saintly bases for these holy days, we can use their sacred blessings in times of spiritual need. Feast days also connect with birth names and confirmation names, with the Feast Day celebrated in place of birthdays in strongly Catholic countries. According to tradition, demons have extreme difficulty working their misfortune on us on our Name Day, especially if we purposefully invoke the saint for protection.

A partial list of Feast Days is therefore useful here, although a comprehensive list is available through the Vatican Library and most local parishes. Those included here feature the more prominent saints, but we should note that the legions of Heaven are filled with many saintly soldiers in the war against the Enemy.

January

3rd St. Genevieve

20th St. Sebastian

21st St. Agnes

28th St. Thomas Aquinas

February

2nd Blessed Virgin Mary, Feast of Purification

3rd St. Blaise

5th St. Agatha

14th St. Valentine

23rd St. Polycarp

March

8th St. John of God

17th St. Patrick

25th Blessed Virgin Mary, Feast of the Annunciation

April

2nd St. Francis of Paola

5th St. Vincent Ferrer

23rd St. George

24th St. Mark

29th St. Catherine of Siena

May

1st St. Joseph

12th St. Pancras

28th St. Bernard of Montjoux

June

1st St. Justin

2nd St. Elmo

9th St. Columba

13th St. Anthony of Padua

29th St. Peter and St. Paul

July

2nd Blessed Virgin Mary, Feast of the Visitation

3rd St. Thomas

11th St. Benedict

22nd St. Mary Magdalene

25th St. Christopher; St. James the Greater

26th St. Anne

27th St. Martha

August

10th St. Laurence

14th St. Maximilian Kolbe

15th Blessed Virgin Mary, Feast of the Assumption

24th St. Bartholomew

27th St. Monica

28th St. Augustine of Hippo

29th St. John the Baptist

September

3rd St. Gregory the Great

8th Blessed Virgin Mary, Feast of the Nativity

21st St. Matthew

27th St. Vincent de Paul

29th St. Gabriel the Archangel, St. Michael the Archangel, St. Raphael the Archangel

30th St. Jerome

October

4th St. Francis of Assisi

17th St. Ignatius of Antioch

18th St. Luke

28 Reverberations: New Directions in the Study of Prayer, St.

Jude

November

11th St. Martin of Tours

15th St. Albert the Great

22nd St. Cecilia

30th St. Andrew

December

4th St. Barbara

6th St. Nicholas of Myra

7th St. Ambrose

8th Blessed Virgin Mary, Feast of the Immaculate Conception

13th St. Lucy

26th St. Stephen

27th St. John the Beloved

Using the Liturgical Calendar in spiritual warfare is an often-overlooked means of amplifying our spiritual power. By beseeching intercessors on their Feast Day—especially if this corresponds with our Name Day, our patron saint, or a Feast of the Blessed Virgin Mary—we can make use of their place in the annual cycle of the Liturgy. As times of sacred reflection, Feast Days allow us to use our prayers and ritual practices to greater effect and summon the strength of Heaven's legions more effectively to our side.

Words from the Saints

Spiritual warfare does not appear often in the words of the saints, who more often than not preach messages of peace, submission, and piety. One notable exception is St. Faustina Kowalska, a Polish Catholic mystic who recorded a vision of Christ in Krakow, Poland, on June 2, 1938. During her beatific vision, Faustina was given 25 secrets of spiritual warfare for her to pronounce to the world. Although largely unknown, Faustina's diary stands as one of the most compelling guides for spiritual warfare in the Catholic tradition, one worth discussing in some detail.

The diary begins by repeating the first words Jesus spoke to Faustina in her vision: "My daughter, I want to teach you about spiritual warfare." From the beginning of her encounter with Christ, Faustina learns that Jesus wants to equip her with the weapons necessary to fight evil in the world and confront the influence of Satan wherever encountered. For example, in Secret 23, Jesus proclaims, "I will not delude you with prospects of peace and consolations; on the contrary prepare for great battle." The image of the meek shepherd is here replaced by Christ the Soldier, much as when in Matthew 10:34 Jesus states, "Do not think that I have come to bring peace to the earth. I have not come to bring peace, but a sword." Scholars have debated this passage for centuries, given that it contradicts Christ's message of peace. On the other hand, in light of Faustina's vision, the image makes sense in that Christ equips us with the weapons necessary to vanquish Satan whenever he rears his hideous head. As the last entry in her diary reads, Jesus says, "Fight like a knight, so I can reward you. Do not be unduly fearful, because you are not alone." The recognition that we are never alone with Christ by our side remains one of our most powerful tools, what Faustina called the Armor of God.

Of course, Faustina is not the only saint to provide us with encouraging words in our battles against evil. Two saints renowned for their ability to exorcize demons are St. John of the Cross and St. Teresa of Avila. As St. Teresa attested of her predecessor, "John of the Cross has a special gift to cast demons," noting that in her town Avila, "he cast many from a person, and he commanded them in the name of God to tell them their names, and they obeyed immediately."[49]

---

[49] (Letter 48.2)

Both Teresa and John of the Cross make it a point to emphasize the devil's tendency "to bring about the downfall of a soul receiving graces from God in prayer than in less-favored souls."[50] In his pride, Satan wants to corrupt those least corrupt souls, which is why those possessed or otherwise under diabolic influence are rarely evil people themselves. St. Teresa, herself one of the holiest mystics in the Tradition, suffered vexations and oppressions throughout her life, including moments of intense doubt, periods when she could not pray due to demonic interference, and temptations toward vile sin.

St. Teresa describes her struggles with the demonic in great detail throughout her writings. Unlike most infernal apparitions, which are invisible and mostly affect the imagination and mind's eye, Teresa also experienced visions of demons externally. "An abominable form; his mouth was horrible," she writes in her autobiography, "Out of his body there seemed to be coming a great flame, which cast no shadow."[51] In another vision, Teresa witnessed two demons with their horns preparing to strangle a priest delivering Mass. Perhaps most intensely, Teresa recounts that in 1550, demons carried her in spirit to Hell itself. Even for Teresa, though, these external visions were rare, and she states: "I have seldom seen him in bodily shape, but I have often seen him without any form, as in the kind of vision I have described, in which no form is seen but the object is known to be there."[52]

---

[50] Moreno (2022), n.p.
[51] *Life*, p. 288
[52] *Life*, p. 292

Another important point made by both St. Teresa and St. John of the Cross is the demonic tendency to exploit our weaknesses. In *The Foundations*, Teresa lists "melancholy" as one such state, now associated with times of anxiety and depression. "The devil knows very well to take advantage of our nature and little understanding," Teresa wrote.[53] Again, Satan is an opportunist. For St. John of the Cross, these weaknesses are exploited by demons through temptation. As he writes in his *Spiritual Canticle*: "The temptation of the devils…is stronger than those of the world and the flesh, because the devils reinforce themselves with these other two enemies, the world and the flesh, in order to wage a rugged war."[54] Demons leverage our weakness to the temptations of the world and our own bodies against us.

St. John of the Cross lists three types of demonic temptation in his *Spiritual Canticle*: those aimed at tricking the imagination; those aimed at distracting the spirit and torturing the body; and "spiritual terrors and horrors."[55] John describes the second temptation in considerable detail, as he himself suffered from physical torments: "the devil more easily disturbs and agitates the spirit with these horrors by means of the senses. The torment and pain he then causes is immense…For since it proceeds nakedly from spirit to spirit the horror the evil spirit causes within the good spirit, if it reaches the spiritual part, is unbearable."[56] Even so, according to John's words, this spiritual

---

[53] Letter to Isabel de S. Jeronimo and Maria de Jesus in *Obras Completas*, 980
[54] *Spiritual Canticle,* p. 431.
[55] *Spiritual Canticle,* p. 476.
[56] *Dark Night,* p. 383.

suffering experienced through the body leads to an ultimately positive spiritual outcome because afterward the "preceding horror of the evil spirit refined the soul so that it could receive this good."[57]

As we've mentioned, temptation constitutes one of Satan's greatest weapons. "As the pilot of the vessel is tried in the storm, as the wrestler is tried in the ring, the soldier in the battle, and the hero in adversity," St. Basil the Great writes, "so is the Christian tried in temptation." The references to storms recall both Noah's trial during the Flood and Jesus' calming of the storm over Galilee, whereas the mention of the wrestler recalls Jacob famously wrestling with an angel in Genesis. St. Basil's words, however, also remind us that temptation is a persistent test of our faith and spiritual perseverance. As St. Anthony the Great puts it, "Expect temptation to your last breath."

We might ask at this point, how can saints, human beings so closely in touch with the Divine, suffer temptation in the way that we do? Archbishop Fulton Sheen points out that Satan actually desires to corrupt those closest to God in a demonstration of his perverse power. "Satan stations more devils on monastery walls than in the dens of iniquity, for the latter offer no resistance." Why would Satan exert extra effort to corrupt those that are already corrupted? The archbishop goes on to say that, "Satan always tempts the pure—the others are already his." This echoes St. Teresa's observation that, "We

---

[57] *Dark Night* p. 385.

always find that those who walked closest to Christ were those who had to bear the greatest trials." Spiritual holiness, therefore, is no guarantee of protection against diabolic interference but in fact too often serves as bait for the Enemy.

Other words from the saints directly address Satan and the demonic threats facing our spiritual lives. The saintly words address several overarching themes: temptation, specific sins, the tactics of the Devil, and opening our hearts to the Word and the Way. Although the saints discuss sin at length, one which they consistently return to is Sloth. "Always be doing something worthwhile," St. Jerome wrote, "then the devil will always find you busy." These words from the saint who gave us the Latin Vulgate bring to mind the oft-repeated saying, "Idle hands are the devil's workshop." St. John Bosco more specifically warns that Sloth is a serious risk for the young: "The principal trap that the devil sets for young people is idleness." St. Anselm, writing centuries earlier, goes even further: "Idleness is the enemy of the soul." As one of the Seven Deadly Sins, Sloth threatens our salvation and tempts us to waste our time on idle pursuits when we could be better directed toward productive action. St. Robert Bellarmine expresses this link between Sloth and temptation and exhorts us to avoid it at all costs: "Flee idleness…for no one is more exposed to such temptations than he who has nothing to do." When we occupy ourselves with good works, spend time with family, and pursue productive hobbies, we inadvertently reduce the risk of temptation and spiritually empower ourselves.

Decrees Against Demonic Operations

Decrees against demonic operations tend to follow the formula laid out in the Gospels, where Christ repeatedly casts out demons from afflicted individuals through a combination of invoking his Father's name and commanding the demonic entity to abandon the body of the possessed. For example, after demonstrating the power of such decrees to his disciples, Jesus states "Go into all the world and preach the gospel to every creature. He who believes will be saved, but he who does not believe will be condemned. And these signs will follow those who believe. In my name they will cast out demons, they will speak with new tongues, they will take up serpents; and if they drink anything deadly, it will by no means hurt them; they will lay hands on the sick and they will recover" (Mark 16:15-18). These holy talents gifted to the disciples are an extension of Christ's power itself, but the gift of casting out demons in his name establishes the basis for the power of the decree.

The Gospel of Mark remains a rich source of decrees against demonic operations. Early in his ministry, Jesus sends the Twelve Apostles out among the people, imparting on them the gifts of healing both spiritual and physical maladies: "And He called the twelve to Him, and began to send them out two by two, and gave them power over unclean spirits…And they cast out many demons, and anointed with oil many who were sick, and healed them" (Mark 6:7-13). Throughout Mark, we find that the power of exorcising "unclean spirits" is linked with the power to heal the sick. However, whereas both exorcism and faith healing share certain ritual similarities—especially the blessing with oil and the laying of hands—casting out demons involves the decree, a practice we saw used to great effect in the contemporary Rite of Major Exorcism. In fact, this parallel runs throughout Matthew and Luke as well, reinforcing the connection between healing the sick and healing the demonically afflicted.

Decrees find their power in the notion of authority, namely the authority of Christ as conqueror of Satan and his agents. As he notes in Luke 10:19, "Behold, I give you the authority to trample on serpents and scorpions, and over all the power of the enemy, and nothing shall by any means hurt you." Both the serpent and the scorpion are symbols of Satan himself, and this verse is yet another basis for the power of the decree in spiritual warfare. In the deserts of the Middle East, the snake and the scorpion present very real physical dangers with their venom, but even more dangerous is the venom of the Dark One, which threatens to poison all of us if we are not prepared with the proper antidotes. Decrees remain one of the strongest remedies, reminding us that Christ provides us with the means to cure ourselves of demonic influence by the sheer authority of his sacrifice and ministry. As John the Evangelist notes, "For this purpose the Son of God was manifested, that He might destroy the works of the devil" (1 John 3:8). When we acknowledge this fact and embrace Christ as our ally in battle, we are practically guaranteed the ultimate victory.

Proven Methods for Consolation and Grace

Sin comes in so many forms that sometimes we are confused about how best to avoid it. As human beings, we will all inevitably sin again and again, no matter how hard we try to do our best and live in the Light. The first step, therefore, is to acknowledge that we can't be perfect, no matter how much we want to be. As John the Evangelist notes, "If we say we have no sin, we deceive ourselves, and the truth is not in us" (1 John 1:8). This admission of honesty is the first step to moving away from sin. Even the saints had their struggles with sin. Consider St. Augustine, who spent his younger years as a drinker, lecher, and gambler until he finally converted to a life of holiness. Even Mother Theresa, one of the most recent examples of saintliness, frequently confessed that she was a sinner. If even the saints struggle with sin, how do we everyday folks stand a chance?

The main goal for us to grow closer to both God and our fellow human beings is spiritual growth, which relies on moral growth. Being moral is more than just determining whether our actions are good or evil because sometimes the distinction isn't that clear. Acts both big and small can carry huge moral consequences, and sometimes it is difficult to see what our actions will ultimately cause. One way to avoid hesitating is to follow a moral code. Only by recognizing a moral code can we even begin to address our own sins. So, in addition to honesty about our sinfulness, the second step to moving closer to God is identifying sin. Fortunately, the Tradition provides several of these codes, which give us rules to live by intended to bring us closer to God and make us better people.

The most obvious code is the Ten Commandments, also known as the Decalogue. Brought down from Mt. Sinai by Moses after the Exodus, these ten rules are considered the most basic laws for society and breaking them is a serious sin. More than simply suggestions, the Commandments are rules that not only improve our relations with others but also strengthen our personal relationship with God. Based on the law noted by Moses in Exodus (20:20-17) and Deuteronomy (5:6-21), the traditional catechetical list of Commandments reads:

1. I am the Lord your God: thou shalt not have strange gods before me.

2. Thou shalt not take the name of the Lord thy God in vain.

3. Remember to keep holy the Lord's Day.

4. Honor thy father and thy mother.

5. Thou shalt not kill.

6. Thou shalt not commit adultery.

7. Thou shalt not steal.

8. Thou shalt not bear false witness against thy neighbor.

9. Thou shalt not covet thy neighbor's wife.

10. Thou shalt not covet thy neighbor's goods.

These rules form the basis of the entire Judaeo-Christian legal system, as well as maintain social order around the world. They also have a profound spiritual dimension as laws that not only bind human communities to each other but also bind human beings to the Divine Order. These laws are not simply rules to live by—they reflect the cosmic laws of the universe laid down by the Creator. Violating these rules not only harms our fellow human beings but is a slight against the Almighty.

Beyond the Commandments, the Old Testament contains lists galore of rules for leading a healthy and holy life. Both Deuteronomy and Leviticus outline these rules in great detail. However, as Jesus notes in the Gospels, "Do not think that I have come to abolish the law or the prophets; I have not come to abolish them but to fulfill them" (Matthew 5:17-18). Even though later writings by St. Paul the Apostle would set aside many older Mosaic Laws, Jesus is very clear that the laws of God are eternal and that violating them is a sure path to sin, which always leads the sinner away from God and closer to the Enemy.

The Covenant between God and Moses, which itself was a renewal of his covenants with Noah and Abraham, was itself renewed through the New Covenant, which "makes the first one obsolete" (Hebrews 8:13).[58] This new Covenant provides us with insight into the redeeming power of Christ in our lives,

---

[58] "In speaking of a new covenant, he makes the first one obsolete. And what is becoming obsolete and growing old is ready to vanish away"

a power capable of dispelling all forms of demonic interference. One of the best expressions of this New Covenant is Paul's Letter to the Romans, which outlines the saving power of grace. The letter discusses sin at length, especially how the grace of God brought by Christ's death and resurrection free us from the power of sin: "For sin will have no dominion over you, since you are not under the law but under grace" (Romans 6:14). When Christ died, a new law replaced the old, making salvation possible through Christ alone instead of relying on the Hebrew Law. As Paul notes, "now we are released from the law, having died to that which held us captive, so that we serve in the new way of the Spirit and not in the old way of the written code" (Romans 7:6). Of course, throughout his ministry, Christ repeatedly stressed the need for people to follow the Commandments. At the same time, He recognized the confusion among many people between what is lawful and what is good. More importantly, as Paul notes, we must know the law to distinguish between good and sinful acts: "What then shall we say? That the law is sin? By no means! Yet if it had not been for the law, I would not have known sin. For I would not have known what it is to covet if the law had not said, 'You shall not covet.'" Paul makes a vital point here for us, namely that it is easy to live in sin if we do not know what defines it. In fact, one of the more common deceptions perpetrated by demons is convincing us that our sinful actions are not wrong, using our ignorance against us.

Another method for avoiding sin's desolation and embracing

consolation is to embrace the Virtues, themselves made all the more real by the presence of temptation. "Virtue is nothing without the trial of temptation," wrote St. Leo the Great, "for there is no conflict without an enemy, no victory without strife." Although not listed outright in the Gospels, the Virtues represent ways of living ethically that embody both Christ's teachings and the path to righteousness. The idea of definitive virtues goes all the way back to Aristotle, who argued in his *Nichomachean Ethics* that virtues were a mean, or average, between two opposing vices of excess and deficiency. For example, the virtue of courage was for Aristotle the golden mean between Foolhardiness and Cowardice. Later Christian writers, such as St. Ambrose and St. Augustine, developed this system further, setting the number of Virtues at seven, the number sacred to God. These Virtues were divided into Four Cardinal Virtues (temperance, justice, prudence, and fortitude) and Three Theological Virtues (faith, hope, and charity). These Virtues represent standards by which to live our lives, each one bringing us closer to the Divine.

Perhaps the most influential version of this system comes from St. Gregory I, who saw the Seven Virtues as the opposites of the Seven Deadly Sins. In Gregory's system, the Seven Virtues are: Chastity (the opposite of Lust), Temperance (the opposite of Gluttony), Charity (the opposite of Greed), Diligence (the opposite of Sloth), Kindness (the opposite of Envy), Patience (the opposite of Wrath), and Humility (the opposite of Pride). This system remains embedded in Church teachings today and provides us with qualities by which to live our lives. They are also certified means of avoiding sin and bringing ourselves closer to God's love. When we practice acts of Charity, for example, we are rebuking Greed. In doing so, we are also embracing Christ's teachings about the dangers of wealth, as in the camel's parable and the needle's eye. This echoes what we read in Proverbs 22:16: "He who oppresses the poor to make more for himself or who gives to the rich, will only come to poverty." We are also embracing Christ's teachings on the Sermon of the Mount, where he lists among the Beatitudes "Blessed are the poor in spirit for they shall inherit the earth." Jesus repeatedly stresses the importance of focusing on the spiritual instead of the material, and the virtues uphold that principle. Lastly, and perhaps most importantly in spiritual warfare, practicing Charity and rejecting Greed allows us to condemn Mammon, the demonic representation of Greed and one of the Princes of Hell. When we refuse to commit the sin of avarice, we, in turn, condemn Mammon and all of his evil influences in the world. "One cannot serve both God and Mammon," Jesus famously stated, and when we practice the Virtue of Charity, we accept the truth of this wisdom. In doing so, our spirits lighten, and God's grace more easily enters our lives.

Breaking Bondages

Bondages can come in many forms. As the Exodus reminds us,

release from bondage represents the highest form of liberation. To be truly free, we must submit. This tenet of Catholicism— submission—was central to the words of Mother Teresa but also forms the central belief of the Islamic tradition. Indeed, Islam itself means "surrender," and the first step to breaking any sort of bondage is to submit oneself to the infinite love of the Creator. Only then can we begin to make ourselves free.

What defines bondage? We may feel bound by our marriage, bound by our career, bound by our relationships. We may feel bound by illness or by illness in a loved one. We may feel bound by our fear of death. All these forms of bondage stem from a single source: fear. In turn, fear often leads to sin.

Sin itself is a form of bondage. When we violate the Commandments, fail to love those around us or fall victim to one of the Deadly Sins, we find ourselves bound by our misdeeds. As we read in Proverbs, "There are six things that the Lord hates, even seven things that are an abomination to Him: haughty eyes, a lying tongue, and hands that shed innocent blood, a heart that devises wicked plans, feet that are swift to run to evil, a false witness who pours out lies, and a person who spreads discord among family members" (6:16-19). Any infraction against the Divine Law leads us toward desolation and away from the possibility of grace. When we uphold the Divine Law that governs the universe by living virtuously, we free ourselves from the bondage of sin and liberate ourselves from Satan's grasp.

Various devotional prayers exist designed to break bondages. One of the best comes from prolific prayer author Sylvia Gunter's *For the Family* (1994), which specifically addresses bondages:

"Father, we come boldly to Your throne of grace, and find mercy and grace to help in time of need. Grant (my loved one) release from bondage to strongholds of the enemy. We plead the blood of Jesus to cancel all commands of the powers of darkness in (my loved one's) life. Jesus came to destroy the works of the devil. His blood defeated the god of this age. In Jesus' name, take back all ground (my loved one) gave the enemy. Draw (my loved one) out of bondage and deception.

We have the heavenly intercession of the Holy Spirit and Jesus. Father, focus the intercession of the Spirit on (my loved one). Answer these prayers according to Your perfect will. Lord Jesus, our Intercessor, apply all Your mighty work against the enemy. Bring all the power of the incarnation, crucifixion, resurrection, and ascension against the assignments seeking to destroy (my loved one). Most High God, contend with those who contend with (my loved one). Rebuke the enemy in all his operations. Dispatch mighty warrior angels to do battle on (my loved one's) behalf.

Send Your light and Your truth and lead (my loved one). Remove all spiritual blindness, deafness, and hardness of heart. Grant (my loved one) eyes to see, ears to hear, and a heart that seeks You. I plead Your mercy and grace over all (my loved one's) personal sin, failure, and family iniquities. Break through and heal (my loved one's) wounded spirit. Bind a hedge of thorns around (my loved one) that will repel all the works of darkness in (my loved one's) life.

This battle is not against flesh and blood, and we have spiritual weapons that set captives free. By Your Holy Spirit break every yoke of bondage in (my loved one's) life. Grant (my loved one) conviction of sin with godly sorrow to repentance and deliverance from captivity. Set (my loved one) completely free. It is written, you shall know the truth and the Truth shall make you free. We are overcome by the blood of the Lamb and by the word of our testimony. Thank You for Your mighty work by the blood of Christ Jesus. Thank you for granting me the grace, power, persistence, and love in intercession with faith for (my loved one) until You are glorified in their life. In Jesus' name. Amen."

This prayer draws upon the full array of Christ and His armies for liberation from bondage. The request for *"release from bondage to strongholds of the enemy"* refers to the passage from Paul's epistles (2 Cor. 10:4). In fact, "strongholds" here is another way of describing bondage as a type of spiritual prison. *We plead the blood of Jesus to cancel all commands of the powers of darkness in (my loved one's) life.*

Fight for Your Children

One of the most devastating forms of demonic interference is those that affect the family. In particular, children are too often casualties in cases of demonic interference. If you find yourself confronting the demonic in your life, take heart in knowing that your children are your legacy, and they too are beloved. Keeping your children safe is crucial, but we must also recognize that Satan can work through young people as well. Cases detailed in the memoirs of exorcists such as Father Amorth occasionally involved children as the afflicted. Most books on spiritual warfare focus on adults, but a recent book by former exorcist Kathleen Beckman, *A Family Guide to Spiritual Warfare: Strategies for Deliverance and Healing* addresses the family. Beckman notes that demonic interference in the family too often goes undefended. Among the tools she introduces are Fearless Faith, Vigilance, and Discernment of Spirits, versions of tools presented in Part 2.

In fact, children are prime targets for Satan's plans because of their innocence. As St. Teresa of Avila reminds us, the devil most often seeks out pure souls because he already has impure ones under his control. Because of their spiritual purity, children sometimes find themselves in the middle of the battle between good and evil. On the one hand, Satan wants to corrupt the purest things above all else. On the other hand, Christ stated in the Scriptures that children are special to God. When the disciples asked Jesus, "Who is the greatest in the kingdom of heaven?" he answered them by bringing a child from the crowd, saying, "Truly, I say to you, unless you turn and become like children, you will never enter the kingdom of heaven" (Mt 18:1-3). The pure in spirit must be like children. But children played more than simply a metaphorical role in Jesus' teachings. As we read in Matthew 19:14, Christ said, "Let the little children come to me, and do not hinder them, for the kingdom of heaven belongs to such as these." Teaching our children to deepen their faith, to read Scripture, and to understand the Tradition are all ways to protect them from demonic threats.

Of course, we must also be careful not to misuse this purity. Accounts from the Middle Ages tell us of an attempt by Christians to march an army of children against their Muslim enemies. Taking place in most versions around AD 1212, this disastrous campaign, known as the Children's Crusade, involved thousands of children in Europe marching to the Holy Land after their mission was blessed by Pope Innocent III. The result was one of the more gruesome examples of misunderstanding Scripture, with massive casualties. Many medieval writers speculated that these campaigns were actually the work of Satan disguised as a holy war. In any event, children should never be used as pawns in spiritual battle, but we must constantly remind ourselves that they are at risk due to their spiritual purity.

Fight for Your Marriage

Marriage is a sacred bond between two souls. As one of the seven sacraments, matrimony allows us to share our spiritual lives with the person we love most in the world. However, no marriage is perfect, and every individual inevitably encounters difficulties living with another person. Especially in a time when divorce is increasingly common, it can be tempting to give up on a marriage. These temptations are precisely the type of demonic interference we must prepare ourselves to fight against. Marriage is the foundation of any family. As a result, demonic forces want nothing more than to undo this foundation and topple the family completely. They may do this through temptations of lust, wrath, and doubt. Try as we might, sometimes our efforts alone are not enough, and we must rely on spiritual intercession to preserve the bond between our partner and us.

St. Paul the Apostle reminds us of the sanctity of marriage in his Letter to the Ephesians. He speaks of the need for wives to be faithful to their husbands and for husbands to "love your wives, just as Christ loved the church and gave himself up for her to make her holy, cleansing her by the washing with water through the word" (Eph. 5:22-26). The love and respect necessary for a successful marriage reflect Christ's love and respect for humanity. More importantly, this love is an act of selflessness. As Paul writes, "husbands ought to love their wives as their own bodies. He who loves his wife loves himself" (Eph. 5:28). Matrimony unites a couple body and soul, and therefore the love nurtured between husband and wife provides spiritual protection for both parties as well.

One useful prayer in this regard is the Marriage Restoration Prayer for those who feel external negative forces threaten their marriage. This prayer invokes direct intercession into the marriage from the divine agency, as well as addressing the concerned parties directly, thereby giving the prayer enhanced potency:

"Lord, I come in the name of Jesus asking that you to make a way in this wilderness of healing and restoration for _____ (name of wife & husband) in their marriage. Lord, that your grace is sufficient to carry them through difficult times, your power is made perfect in their weaknesses, and the power of Christ is in them. As Christians, greater is You that is in _____ (name of wife & husband) than the evil one in the world because your power is greater than the power of Satan and all who do his work. I am so thankful that You are watching to make certain that your Word is fulfilled and that You are performing it in our marriage. Thank you that you will complete the work that you started in this marriage. O Sovereign LORD, you are God! Your words are trustworthy, and you have promised these good things to me. You have said that You will build a home for them and that it pleases You to bless their marriage so it will continue before You forever. You have spoken, and with your blessing, this home and marriage will be established with blessings forever.

Lord, I pray that you will allow healing and reconciliation to take place. That whatever hurts or disappointments they have experienced can be mended through the power of your undying, eternal Love. We realize, Father, that they cannot change anything that has happened. But, they can go forth together, keeping, renewing, and once again honoring their vows. We ask that you endow them with wisdom to endure and a tongue that speaks healing, restoration, & peace.

Abba, I ask that you would mend their hearts closely together and be the center of their marriage. Lord, we ask that they seek forgiveness for any wrongdoing. We pray that they extend love and patience to one another and that the lines of communication, sensitivity as well as understanding are once again opened. We ask that you will allow all the pain, hurt, and disappointment to begin to subside. Lord, we ask that forgiveness is welcomed by each of them. Lord, we ask that you would allow your JOY to flow once again from heart to heart between them. Father, we ask that you direct them as they seek you first in building trust, transparency, and intimacy. Father, we pray peace over their household, in the name of Jesus, Amen."

Another version of this prayer is intended for us to pray when our own marriage is suffering troubles. Again, whether or not these troubles are the result of demonic interference, these prayers provide us with a means of healing wounds between our partners and us through our faith:

"Almighty Father, You are omniscient, omnipotent, and able to do things that are impossible for man. I humble myself before you today, Lord, and ask you to restore my marriage. Please bring my wife/husband back to me so that we can fulfill Your word that those whom You have joined together let no man put asunder. Forgive me for my part of sin in this separation, and show me what I need to do to restore my relationship with You and my relationship with her/him. I Pray, O Lord, to reunite us in Jesus' name. Please have mercy upon us, O God, and I will always be thankful to You for restoring my marriage. I ask for the forgiveness of our sins. I pray for all those people who may have come in between our relationship

that you would set them on the right path and reveal to them the truth of your Word. I freely offer my forgiveness to them for their part in this separation. Fill us all with your Holy Spirit and guide us into your truth. I forgive my spouse for all the past hurt and pain and pray that you would cleanse my mind and my heart from carrying any thoughts that are not from you, in Jesus' Name, Amen."

When we implore God to help in our marriage, we ask Him to intercede against any demonic forces polluting this holy bond. Few things are more traumatic than marital discord, especially if it leads the couple toward divorce. When a home is sundered in such a way, Satan and his demonic minions have all the more opportunity to infiltrate the family and cause further havoc. As a sacrament, Matrimony occupies a central place in the Tradition, and Satan in his pride wants nothing more than to corrupt the sacred. Just as the serpent tempted Eve to disobey her Father and Adam, so too does the risk of chaos exist in every marriage. Through prayer, meditation, and virtuous living, couples can strengthen their connection with each other and their connection with the Divine.

Fight for Your Health

Demonic interference often targets our body in an attempt to weaken our spirit. As we saw in our discussion of exorcism and possession, demons take over the body, not the spirit, when they possess an individual. Perhaps more importantly, the decrees and Scriptural power focused on casting out demons nearly always come along with the power to heal sickness. In today's age of medical science, we often find ourselves dismissing illness as a purely physical problem. But the fact is, physical illness is oftentimes a result of spiritual and mental distress and most often a combination of all three factors. When the spirit is sick, the body follows. Physical sickness is also a test of our faith, as it is easy to fall into despair when our bodies begin to fail us.

Specific prayers for health are among the most useful in the canon. Some focus on healing ourselves when we face illness; others are targeted at others suffering from ailments. One powerful defense against the maladies brought on by demonic forces is the novena, particularly the Novena of St. Jude and the Novena of St. Peregrine. These nine-day prayer rituals may or may not involve fasting, but the purpose is the same: to ask for intercession from these two saints—patrons of those diagnosed with cancer—and heal the body. Although cancer is a medical diagnosis, the cause itself can often be one of demonic influence, such as obsessive smoking habits, alcoholism, drug use, or other addictions that often have a demonic component in addition to their medical ones.

Fight for Your Livelihood

Concern over one's business or career is normal. Challenges

arise that pressure our finances and drive us to doubt our faith. However, this challenge is by no means new. A large number of assurances in Scripture provide us with advice on how to handle these problems, especially those brought on by demonic influence. Whether we are facing decisions about whether to put profit above people, struggling with temptations to cheat our way out of debts, or envying the success of others while our own career falters, the righteous path is the only one that provides us with the necessary protection against the temptations of Satan and his fallen angels.

Consider Proverbs 24:3-4, which reminds us that "Through wisdom a house is built, and by understanding it is established; and by knowledge the rooms shall be filled with all precious and pleasant riches." In fact, Proverbs is full of excellent suggestions for how to conduct ourselves in business. Proverbs warns against deceitful business practices, which themselves can invite demonic interference in our lives. Every time we transgress in such a way, we provide a door for the demonic. As we read in Proverbs, "A false balance is an abomination to the Lord, but a just weight is His delight" (11:1). The emphasis on honest labor throughout the Bible is our guide for how to live our lives. If we remember the power of Virtues as a means of strengthening our relationship with God, we understand that the virtues of Diligence and Temperance protect us against the demonic influence of their sinful opposites, Sloth and Gluttony. These same principles apply in our careers, in how we conduct business and treat our co-workers.

141

One of the greatest threats to our professional success is, therefore, Sloth. The temptation to procrastinate or divert our attention from our work is constant in today's media-saturated world. To truly protect ourselves against these temptations, we must remember that the "soul of the sluggard craves and gets nothing, but the soul of the diligent is made fat" (Proverbs 13:4). This extends to honesty in our careers. The demonic temptation to lie, cheat, and steal in our business dealings remains a persistent one, but we must remember that "Wealth obtained by fraud dwindles, but the one who gathers by labor increases it" (Proverbs 13:11). The old adage about actions speaking louder than words is an understatement in this regard because true success in business demands honesty, integrity, and faith that no matter the circumstances, the Lord will provide. We find a similar warning in Deuteronomy: "You shall not have in your bag differing weights, a large and a small. You shall not have in your house differing measures, a large and a small. You shall have a full and just weight; you shall have a full and just measure, that your days may be prolonged in the land which the Lord your God gives you" (25:13-15). Honesty in all dealings, whether personal or professional, is always the best policy since Satan, the Prince of Lies, constantly seeks to tempt us toward deceit.

The Book of Malachi goes even further, equating such deceit with the sins of sorcery and oppression: "Then I will draw near to you for judgment; and I will be a swift witness against the sorcerers and against the adulterers and against those who swear falsely, and against those who oppress the wage earner in his wages, the widow and the orphan, and those who turn aside the alien and do not fear Me, says the Lord of hosts" (Malachi 3:5). In the New Testament, some of the best advice in this regard comes from Luke 16:10, where we read: "He who is faithful in a very little thing is faithful also in much; and he who is unrighteous in a very little thing is unrighteous also in much." In other words, even the slightest amount of faith can lead to significant positive change in our professional lives. When we live virtuously, as Christ taught us to live, we reap the benefits of spiritual strength and often professional and financial success.

Other examples from Scripture urge just dealings as the best way to prevent demonic interference in our careers. We are encouraged to cooperate with those in our community rather than view them as opponents or competitors: "You shall not oppress your neighbor, nor rob him. The wages of a hired man are not to remain with you all night until morning" (Leviticus 19:13). The Commandments against covetousness and theft apply in business as well, as do the Virtues of Charity and Temperance. There may be no arena besieged by more demonic attacks than business, especially in this age of global corporations and materialism.

PART 4

Arsenal Scriptures, Deliverance Prayers, and Invocations

Scriptures Verses for Warfare

We cannot underestimate the sheer power of Scripture in spiritual warfare. As the embodied Word of God, the Scriptures offer us a direct line of communication from the Divine to the human. When we recite from Scripture, we are literally reciting God's revelations to his children. Each passage is infused with His Grace and serves as a potential weapon against the Evil One. As St. Paul reminds us, when confronted with evil in our lives, we must equip "the sword of the Spirit, which is the word of God" (Eph. 6:17).

Although the Catechism prefers the New Testament, the Old Testament also contains passages effective for anyone confronting demonic interference. In particular, the books of Ezekiel and Isaiah contain many passages directly addressing ways to repel evil energies. Genesis and Exodus are also fertile sources for verses that might act as weapons for us. A favorite among practicing exorcists is the Books of Psalms, an ancient and potent source of spiritual wisdom.

In the New Testament, all four Gospels provide excellent verses, though the Pauline Epistles and other letters—especially those of the Apostles—offer another set of possibilities. In some instances, a single verse is enough to fend off evil influence. In more serious cases of obsession, vexation, possession, or infestation, more extensive readings are necessary.

Old Testament

The first five books of the Bible, sometimes called the Pentateuch, provide us with several powerful verses for use in spiritual warfare. Genesis contains a series of stories in many ways closest to the Creator. Throughout Genesis, despite humanity's continued failures, God renews his vow as protector and source of all virtue. When Adam and Eve are cast out of Eden for disobeying the only law of the Garden, God does not abandon them. When Noah proves himself the only man faithful enough to be spared from the Flood, God renews this vow through a Covenant to watch over Noah's descendants, which includes all of us.

Several verses from Genesis specifically address the opposite functions of blessings and curses. As we discussed in Part 1, oftentimes curses are a gateway to demonic influence and involve the associated negative energy, but some curses in the Bible actually call upon God to inflict his wrath on our enemies. One of the primary reminders we find in Genesis is that all blessings ultimately come from God. In Genesis 12:3 we read: "And I will bless them that bless thee, and curse him that curseth thee: and in thee shall all families of the earth be blessed." This verse's reciprocal formula for blessings and curses is important because it demonstrates God's supreme justice. In all things, God represents Order, whereas Satan and his fallen angels are agents of chaos. We encounter a similar passage later in the same book: "Let people serve thee, and nations bow down to thee: be lord over thy brethren, and let thy mother's sons bow down to thee: cursed be everyone that curseth thee, and blessed be he that blesseth thee" (Genesis 27:29). In other words, God is always on our side as long as we maintain an open heart. Our enemies and those who persecute us, both human and demonic, are, in turn, his enemies.

The Book of Exodus likewise reinforces the human connection with God's Covenant, reestablished in his promise to Moses on Mount Sinai through the Ten Commandments and later through the Law handed down in the Book of Deuteronomy and the Book of Leviticus. Both Deuteronomy and Leviticus, in particular, provide us with verses from Scripture that directly address the threat of the demonic. In Deuteronomy, God speaks through Moses to assure us that He will protect us from our enemies: "And the Lord thy God will put all these curses upon thine enemies, and on them that hate thee, which persecuted thee" (30:7). Deuteronomy makes specific references to the threat of demonic interference. As we read in Deuteronomy 18:9-13: "When you come into the land which the Lord your God is giving you, you shall not learn to imitate the abominations of the people there. Let there not be found among you anyone who immolates his son or daughter in the fire, nor a fortune teller, soothsayer, charmer, diviner, or caster of spells, nor one who consults ghosts and spirits or seeks oracles from the dead. Anyone who does such things is an abomination to the Lord . . . You, however, must be altogether sincere toward the Lord, your God." The central warning in this verse is that seeking influence or supernatural power by means outside of the Divine is a path toward the demonic. The "abominations of the people there" refers to the pagan practices in Canaan before the arrival of the Israelites, but more properly this warning applies to demonic entities as they were associated with these pre-Israelite deities. More importantly, the verse condemns the various abhorrent practices associated with these demons, including human sacrifice, divination, and necromancy. Although most of these practices are obsolete today, we must note that this does not condemn all forms of these practices, but only those achieved through means not involving the Divine. That is to say, communicating with our ancestors through prayer or votive offerings is permissible, even encouraged, so long as we do so through sacred channels and not through some unholy power. Similarly, asking God for help in some future endeavor or to give us insight into the righteous path is a form of divination, but one that uses God as the source rather than cards, stars, or palms. These practices can be safely undertaken if we do so with the acknowledgment that all Truth comes from a single divine source.

Similar injunctions can be found in the Book of Leviticus. We find in Leviticus 19:31 a warning against fortune telling: "Do not go to mediums or consult fortune tellers, for you will be defiled by them. I, the Lord, am your God." Later in Leviticus 20:6, we encounter a similar warning: "Should anyone turn to mediums and fortune tellers and follow their wanton ways, I will turn against such a one and cut him off from his people." Again, these proscriptions are intended to warn us against seeking answers outside of God. The soothsayers condemned in these passages are those that attempted to glimpse the future with the help of demonic powers, not through the benevolence of Grace. Today, many mediums, fortune tellers, and curanderas practice their craft through the lens of the Christian tradition. This is especially true of curanderas in Hispanic cultures, where the fortuneteller or seer is operating through divine channels, not demonic ones.

The Book of Psalms provides one of the most effective sources for Old Testament verses useful in spiritual combat. In fact, many of the verses contained in the *Rituale Romanum* for use in the Rite of Major Exorcism come from Psalms. These words come from the spiritual meditations of King David, whose son Solomon became an expert on protection against demonic entities. In practice, psalms are meant to be sung or chanted, a tradition mentioned by St. Paul the Apostle in his letters to the Ephesians (5:19) and Colossians (3:16). Several centuries later, St. Augustine of Hippo encouraged the singing of psalms in his *Confessions* as a means of amplifying the power of prayer (IX:6-14; X:33-49).

Psalms provide us with several benedictions to protect ourselves from Satan in his role as destroyer. We read in Psalm 107 that we need only ask for divine protection, and we will receive it: "Send Your Word, and deliver me from any destruction. (Ps 107:20). In Psalm 108, David offers up his song in praise of God while also asking for help against the interferences of the demonic. After requesting God's blessing for humanity, David sings, "Give us aid against the enemy, for the help of man is worthless. With God we will gain victory, and he will trample down our enemies" (Ps. 108: 12-13). David's psalms frequently remind us that we are not alone in our fights against the demonic. Indeed, we have the most powerful ally of all if we open our hearts to Him.

Psalm 109 is perhaps the most effective verse in the Book for spiritual warfare. This psalm functions as a sacred curse against those enacting evil upon us, "wicked and deceitful men" (Ps. 109: 2). In this psalm, David invokes God's power as supreme judge to punish those working for satanic ends, asking for the

Lord to "Appoint an evil man [or the Evil One] to oppose him; let an accuser [or Satan] stand at his right hand. When he is tried, let him be found guilty" (Ps. 109: 6-7). This verse presents us with an instance where Satan is acting as a punisher on God's behalf, literally turning against those who would follow him. This inversion demonstrates just how much power God wields over the Enemy. In many ways, Psalm 109 functions as a counter-curse, intended to turn misfortunes against those who would curse us. David goes on to list a variety of punishments to be inflicted on those against whom this psalm is directed: barrenness, debt, isolation. The target of this psalm is in effect cut off from the bounty of God: "May their sins always remain before the Lord…He loved to pronounce a curse—may it come to him; he found no pleasure in blessing—may it be far from him. He wore cursing as his garment; it entered into his body like water, into his bones like oil. May it be like a cloak wrapped about him, like a belt tied forever around him" (Ps. 109: 15-19). David's words rank among the harshest rebukes of evil in the Bible, but they also remind us that those who seek to harm us through demonic means will face divine justice. Unlike the Deadly Sin of Wrath, the Divine Wrath invoked by David in Psalm 109 takes as its target all corrupted and evil actions and people, preserving order in the face of chaos.

The Prophetic Books

The Book of Isaiah remains central in the Catholic tradition because Christ fulfilled so many of the prophecies foretold by Isaiah. Written during the Babylonian Captivity, the words of Isaiah are ones of both hope for those aligned with God and doom for those who stand against Him. Isaiah (14:12-15) directly refers to the origin of demons:

How you have fallen from heaven,

O morning star, son of the dawn!

You have been cast down to the earth,

You who once laid low the nations!

You said in your heart,

'I will ascend to heaven;

I will raise my throne

above the stars of God;

I will sit enthroned on the mount of

assembly,

On the utmost heights of the sacred

mountain.

I will ascend above the tops of the

clouds;

I will make myself like the Most

High.'

But you are brought down to the

grave,

to the depths of the pit.'

This passage contains the story of Lucifer's pride and fall, but also warns us against the threats of pride in our own lives. Many Biblical scholars recognize that Isaiah here is referring to both Lucifer and the proud Babylonian king Sargon, who conquered and enslaved the Jewish people. The parable serves as an authoritative reminder that pride, one of the Seven Deadly Sins and the domain of Satan, weakens our spirits and makes us more vulnerable to demonic influence. As discussed in Part 1, Satan wants us to be proud like him because he can more easily infiltrate our lives.

Perhaps the most relevant passage from Isaiah refers explicitly to spiritual warfare: "See, it is I who created the blacksmith who fans the coals into flame and forges a weapon fit for its work. And it is I who have created the destroyer to work havoc; no weapon forged against you will prevail, and you will refute every tongue that accuses you." (54:16-17). This passage, rich in symbolism, reminds us of several crucial facts. First, God as omniscient Creator is Himself the ultimate source of even Satan and his demons. Although this seems contradictory, it reminds us that God's plan reaches far beyond the limits of our human understanding. Second, God allowed Satan to proceed with his evil workings in many ways to test our own spiritual strength. When we recognize temptation and reject it, we, in turn, reject Satan and move closer to God in an act of consolation. Third, this passage reminds us that with the weapons of God, both word and deed, we are invincible to evil. This belief is echoed in a Catholic prayer against demonic attack that draws on Isaiah's words: "Father, your word said that no weapon formed against me will prosper, I canceled and destroyed all demonic weapons set against me and my household in Jesus's name."[59] Even though it is a brief invocation, this link between the Old and New Testaments makes this prayer especially effective in spiritual warfare.

New Testament Verses

The New Testament overflows with Scriptural resources for spiritual warfare situations. Six of the New Testament's twenty-seven books come to us directly from the Apostles, including the Gospels of St. Matthew and St. John, letters from St. James,

---

[59] Several sources for this prayer exist, and it is included in various forms in the *Rituale Romanum*, deliverance prayer books, and suggested in the Rite of Minor Exorcism.

St. Peter, and St. Jude, and the epistles of St. Paul.[60] The New Testament also provides us with useful verses from the Acts of the Apostles and the Book of Revelation, which concerns the End of Days. Many of these verses we have already discussed, especially the Gospel accounts of Jesus performing exorcisms.

The Gospels themselves provide us with the most direct link to the words and deeds of Christ and therefore function as the best weapons available to us. An especially powerful balm against evil influence comes to us through the Beatitudes. The Sermon on the Mount remains perhaps Jesus' greatest teaching moment. Delivered on the Mount of Olives outside Jerusalem, the Sermon contains the essence of Christ's mission as well as insights into Christian virtue. The Beatitudes remind us that our role as servants of the Light relies not on any earthly power or material wealth but instead on our willingness to serve others and thereby serve God. Those extolled by Christ in the Beatitudes are not the wealthy or powerful or pontificating frauds, but rather those who society too often tramples in the rat race to dominate others. Instead of seeking domination, Jesus teaches us to pursue the righteous path instead and acknowledge those less fortunate than us. In the Gospel of Matthew (5:2-12), Jesus delivers the Beatitudes as a series of

---

[60] We should note here that St. Paul, often referred to as St. Paul the Apostle, was not one of the original Twelve and did not in fact know Jesus during his lifetime. Paul's conversion on the road to Damascus is one of the most famous in the canon, recounting how Paul (then called Saul) encountered the resurrected Christ and afterwards became his most fervent disciple. The spread of Christianity throughout the Greco-Roman world is largely the result of Paul's efforts.

proverbs:

Blessed are the poor in spirit, for theirs is the kingdom of Heaven.

Blessed are those who mourn, for they will be comforted.

Blessed are the meek, for they shall inherit the earth.

Blessed are those you hunger and thirst after righteousness, for they shall be filled.

Blessed are the merciful, for they shall be shown mercy.

Blessed are the pure of heart, for they shall see God.

Blessed are the peacemakers, for they shall be called the sons of God.

Blessed are those who are persecuted because of righteousness, for theirs is the kingdom of Heaven.

Blessed are you when people insult you, persecute you and falsely say all kinds of evil against you because of me. Rejoice and be glad, because great is your reward in Heaven, for in the same way they persecuted the prophets who came before you.

The Beatitudes represent an upending of the usual order of things in the Biblical world, an order that remains part of the status quo today. When most people think of success, they think of wealth, influence, and other forms of "power," neglecting to recognize that true power is giving these things up to pursue a higher spiritual power. Each beatitude overturns assumptions about the world. Instead of blessing the strong-willed, Jesus blesses those who are "poor in spirit," meaning anyone facing spiritual crisis or doubt. He reassures them that a far greater reward awaits them if they follow the Way. When we recognize our own spiritual weakness, we can then strengthen ourselves. Rather than praising conquerors, Jesus blesses "those who mourn," drawing attention to the fact that no matter how much we gain materially in life, we all must face the stark reality of our own mortality. By doing so through mourning, we not only respect the deceased but also turn our eyes toward the greater realities of life and death. Instead of praising the brash and proud, Jesus blesses "the meek," those who practice humility and submit to the Divine Will.

Jesus does not only bless the outcasts, however, also reserving praise for those who live by the code of his teaching. Whereas too often people attempt to make gains through sheer force, Jesus blesses those who "hunger and thirst after righteousness," pointing out that ultimately justice comes to all human beings. Those who live their lives in the awareness of the ultimate Good, which comes through the Creator, will find themselves in a higher state of spiritual Grace. In a world so frequently plagued with cruelty, whether through war, crime, or the smaller cruelties of daily life, Jesus blesses "the merciful." This beatitude is especially important because it reminds us that the core of Christ's teachings—and a fundamental virtue that protects us from the potential of demonic influence—is the paramount need for forgiveness. This includes forgiving not only those who wrong us but also to have mercy on others for their shortcomings. This mercy, of course, extends to us as well. Unless we forgive ourselves for our sins, both great and small, we make ourselves more vulnerable to the workings of Satan and his operatives. Through practicing the virtue of mercy, we live as Christ lives, which itself strengthens our spiritual defenses. With so much negative energy in the world, it is easy to become cynical and let our hearts grow heavy with doubt. Jesus reminds us in the sixth beatitude that those "pure of heart" shall see God. Purity of heart encompasses a range of traits, the virtues above all. Through the practices of the Four Cardinal Virtues of temperance, justice, prudence, and fortitude, and the Three Theological Virtues of faith, hope, and charity, our hearts are purified. Similarly, by following the Commandments, honoring the Sacraments, and practicing the Word through deeds, our heart cleanses itself of sin. As a result, demonic entities find those pure of heart far more difficult to corrupt than those whose hearts remain callous and corrupt.

In a world besieged by warfare, the seventh beatitude is especially important. When Jesus blesses peacemakers, he calls us to confront and condemn warfare wherever we encounter it. However, warfare can come in many forms. Political warfare continues to shake the globe: the persistent struggles in the Middle East in Yemen, Syria, and Iran; the tragic wars in the former Soviet Union territories of Ukraine, Chechnya, and Georgia; the threat of war surrounding China's claims to Taiwan, or political upheavals in African countries such as the

Democratic Republic of the Congo, Chad, or Sudan. All these ongoing conflicts, many of which have roiled for decades, tempt us to think that warfare is simply a fact of life. Jesus instead calls on us to recognize that war rarely solves the underlying problems that cause it and that peace shall always remain the superior choice. As we read in Revelation, one of the Four Horsemen of the Apocalypse is War.[61] Ultimately, through the restorative effect of Christ's victory at the Rapture, the Horseman of War himself faces defeat, paving the way for the eternal peace of the Kingdom of God. This hope for peace rests at the core of Jesus' teaching.

The last Beatitude addresses the persecuted. Although Jesus is primarily referring to those persecuted for their belief in Him and His teachings, this Beatitude applies to all people persecuted by any form of oppression. This includes those persecuted because of their color or creed, political prisoners, and those persecuted because of mental or physical disability. In His role as Good Shepherd, Jesus is offering his benevolent protection to those facing such hardships. Indeed, Christ faces the ultimate persecution and sympathizes with anyone bearing their own personal Cross.

This Beatitude was especially vital in the earliest days of the Church when Christians were regularly persecuted, tortured,

---

[61] The Four Horsemen—Pestilence, Famine, War, and Death—are harbingers of the End of Times and therefore servants of the Red Dragon (a manifestation of Satan). Although we are never explicitly told that they are demons, their position as powerful agents of destruction suggest that they can be considered demonic.

and executed throughout the Roman Empire. Images of martyrs facing terrible punishments, humiliation, and death because they chose to follow the righteous path instead of giving up. Even Jesus' closest disciples—such as St. Peter and St. Andrew, his first two apostles—faced humiliating and gruesome persecutions. St. Peter, recognized as the first pope in the Catholic tradition, was crucified on an inverted cross in a mockery of the Crucifixion. Similarly, his brother St. Andrew was crucified on a cross shaped like an X, an ironic twist given that "X" or "chi" is the first letter of Christ in Greek. The first martyr, St. Stephen, was stoned to death, and another early martyr, St. Sebastian, was tied to a post and riddled with arrows. Centuries later, St. Joan of Arc was burnt at the stake. All these hagiographic stories remind us that believing in goodness and practicing the teachings of Christ can sometimes pit us against society. Rather than submit, we must remain resolute in our belief and continue to wear the Armor of God as protection against enemies, whether human or superhuman. For this reason, and by virtue of their righteous suffering, the martyrs remain powerful intercessors in spiritual warfare situations.

The Beatitudes serve as a manual for opening our eyes to the suffering of others and call us to a life of charity. Acts of charity by their very nature reject the temptations of Greed, represented by the demon Mammon, and repel the desires to privilege wealth over all else. They call us to practice peace and love in a world too often bombarded by war and hatred. In our modern times, many people have either forgotten the Beatitudes or rejected them, instead pursuing what the philosopher Nietzsche once called "the will to power" and "master morality." In his book *The Genealogy of Morality*, Nietzsche rejects Christ's teachings as praising "slave morality" and encouraging us to see weaknesses as virtues. However, Nietzsche is largely missing the point, as are those who follow his thinking, consciously or not. In the Beatitudes, Jesus is not urging us to be weak but instead to protect and respect those less fortunate than us. Furthermore, the Beatitudes call upon us to recognize our human weaknesses, whether poverty of spirit or a temptation towards the sins of pride.

The Book of the Acts of the Apostles, or Acts, concerns the deeds of the apostles after the Ascension. The latter half of the book concerns the conversion and ministry of St. Paul. A verse from Paul's conversion narrative gives us a useful invocation, first spoken by Ananias of Damascus when he cured Paul of his blindness after witnessing the transfigured Christ. Laying his hands on Paul, Ananias states, "Brother Saul, the Lord, Jesus, that appeared unto thee in the way as thou camest, hath sent me, that though mightest receive thy sight, and be filled with the Holy Spirit" (Acts 9:17). A similar formula can be used in spiritual warfare by replacing Paul's name with the intended benefact, the prayer conferring the blessing of the Holy Spirit. The parallels with curing blindness also link this verse with a spiritual unblinding, opening the spiritual eye of the blessed to the power of the Divine.

Conversely, Acts gives us a tool for blinding demons and their agents. In Acts 13, we read of Paul's encounter in Paphos with "a Jewish sorcerer and false prophet named Bar-Jesus" (13:6). We learn that this false prophet was operating under demonic influence, so Paul curses him: "You are a child of the devil and an enemy of everything that is right! You are full of different kinds of deceit and trickery. Will you never stop perverting the right way of the Lord? Now the hand of the Lord is against you. You are going to be blind, and for a time you will be unable to see the light of the sun" (Acts 13: 10-11). Paul's words are likewise effective against demonic entities and their agents. In fact, Paul's injunction closely parallels the various prayers against the Evil Eye discussed later in this part. It is important to note here that blinding a demon or their agents as a practice traces its origins back to this episode early in Paul's ministry.

Another encounter between Paul and the demonic occurred in Philippi, where Paul and his companion St. Barnabas find themselves heckled by a servant girl who earned money for her masters by soothsaying. Realizing the girl is possessed by an evil force, Paul "became so troubled that he turned around and said to the spirit, 'In the name of Jesus Christ, I command you to come out of her!' At that moment the spirit left her" (Acts 16:16-24). This episode not only echoes Christ's many expulsions of evil spirits in the Gospels, but also parallels the formula of exorcism in the Major Rite, particularly the imperative formula whereby the exorcist directly addresses the demonic entity. Another aspect of this episode is that Paul and

161

Barnabas face imprisonment for their actions, reminding us that oftentimes in spiritual warfare, we must prepare ourselves to face backlash, both from the demonic entities involved and those unwilling to believe in the power of the Spirit.

The Pauline Epistles, some of the earliest known Christian writings, also strengthen us throughout the New Testament. More than any other individual, St. Paul is responsible for the spread of the Word throughout the Greco-Roman world. The letters that come down to us in the New Testament are part of this legacy and connect us to the earliest days of the Faith. Paul's letters give us the earliest full expression of Christ's teaching. The Apostle includes many instructions for how to lead a holier life and how to confront demonic presences attempting to distract us from the righteous path.

In his Letter to the Romans, Paul reminds us that God's love for us is infinite and that not even demons can truly separate us from it: "No, in all these things we are more than conquerors through him who loved us. For I am convinced that neither death nor life, neither angels nor demons, neither the present nor the future, nor any powers, neither height nor depth, nor anything else in all creation, will be able to separate us from the love of God that is in Christ Jesus our Lord" (8:37-39). Paul here is reassuring us that Christ embodies God's love, a love which no power can undo. Even though we may fall into temptation or lose faith, we always have a path to return to God.

Perhaps the most valuable Pauline Epistle for spiritual warfare is the Second Letter to the Corinthians. This Scripture is a testament to forgiveness, both our own forgiving of others and the Lord's forgiveness of us. This forgiveness is transcendent, fortifying us against the devil's wiles. As Paul writes, "If you forgive anyone, I also forgive him. And what I have forgiven— if there was anything to forgive—I have forgiven in the sight of Christ for your sake, in order that Satan might not outwit us. For we are not unaware of his schemes" (2 Cor. 2: 10-11). Here Paul gives us clear insight into the power of forgiveness as a weapon against Satan.

Paul also reminds us of the power of proclaiming our faith. He writes, "We are not like Moses, who would put a veil over his face to keep the Israelites from gazing at it while the radiance was fading away. But their minds were made dull, for to this day the same veil remains when the old covenant is read. It has not been removed, because only in Christ is it taken away...whenever anyone turns to the Lord, the veil is taken away" (2 Cor. 3:13-16). When we embrace Christ as Savior, we too become like Moses, who gazed upon the Face of God on Mount Sinai. Unlike Moses, however, Paul tells us not to wear a veil but instead to let our experience of divine encounter shine outward for all to see, including the agents of Satan.

Paul also praises suffering as a means of spiritual empowerment. Regardless of the trials we face, we must remember that "as servants of God we commend ourselves in every way: in great endurance; in troubles, hardships and distresses; in beatings, imprisonments and riots; in hard work, sleepless nights and hunger" (2 Cor. 6:4-6). Therefore, any trouble we encounter in life is, as Paul reminds us, a test of faith—and anytime we pass such a test, we resist Satan's attempts to take advantage of our weaknesses. On the contrary, when we uphold the will of God through "purity, understanding, patience and kindness; in the Holy Spirit and in sincere love; in truthful speech and in the power of God; with weapons of righteousness in the right hand and in the left," our spirits are made capable of withstanding anything life throws at us. We must think of our own suffering in light of Christ's sacrifice, which Paul describes beautifully as "God made him who had no sin to be sin for us, so that in him we might become the righteousness of God" (2 Cor. 5: 21). When we confront the demonic in our own lives, this acknowledgment of our role as God's righteousness empowers us as agents of Light.

As agents of Light, we are soldiers against darkness. Paul reminds us of this when he warns us not to stray toward disbelief: "Do not be yoked together with unbelievers. For what do righteousness and wickedness have in common? Or what fellowship can light have with darkness? What harmony is there between Christ and Belial?" (2 Cor. 6:14-15). In other words, when we take up the path of righteousness, we, as a consequence, become natural enemies of darkness and all its operatives. The reference to Belial, one of the principal demons in Satan's armies, testifies to Paul's knowledge that righteousness is toxic to the demonic.

The end of Paul's letter is both a reassurance of our spiritual arsenal and a warning against deceitful spirits. He assures us that even though we inhabit this world, "weapons we fight with are not the weapons of the world. On the contrary, they have divine power to demolish strongholds" (2 Cor. 10:4). The weapons of righteousness—prayer, faith, good deeds—allow us to fend off those infernal enemies seeking to corrupt us. At the same time, Paul warns us about "false apostles": "I am afraid that just as Eve was deceived by the serpent's cunning, your minds may somehow be led astray from your sincere and pure devotion to Christ...For such men are false apostles, deceitful workmen, masquerading as apostles of Christ. And no wonder, for Satan himself masquerades as an angel of light. It is not surprising, then, if his servants masquerade as servants of righteousness" (2 Cor. 11:3-14). As we mentioned in our discussion of demonic tactics, oftentimes, demons will present themselves as holy. As creatures of deception, they will use any means necessary to trick us into believing their lies. If we recognize them, however, they can wield no power over us.

Like Corinthians, Paul's Letter to the Ephesians contains many valuable spiritual insights, but it is the sixth chapter that explains the "Armor of God," one of the greatest tools at our disposal in any spiritual combat. Paul implores us: "...be strong in the Lord and in his mighty power. Put on the full armor of God, so that you can take your stand against the devil's schemes. For our struggle is not against flesh and blood, but against the rulers, against the authorities, against the powers of this dark world and against the spiritual forces of evil in the heavenly realms. Therefore, put on the full armor of God, so that when the day of evil comes, you may be able to stand your ground, and after you have done everything, to stand. Stand firm then, with the belt of truth buckled around your waist, with the breastplate of righteousness in place, and with your feet fitted with the readiness that comes from the gospel of peace. In addition to all this, take up the shield of faith, with which you can extinguish all the flaming arrows of the evil one. Take the helmet of salvation and the sword of the Spirit, which is the word of God. And pray in the Spirit on all occasions with all kinds of prayers and requests. With this in mind, be alert and always keep on praying for all the Lord's people" (Eph. 6:12-17).

A final verse from Paul comes to us in his Letter to the Hebrews. Here, Paul makes a point to emphasize the dominance of Christ over Satan, writing, "Since therefore the children share in flesh and blood, He Himself likewise partook of the same nature, that through death He might destroy him who has the power of death, that is, the Devil" (2:14). This verse can be used in spiritual combat to remind demonic entities that they are powerless in the presence of Christ. That presence comes through us when we confront any and all evil. Satan has no absolute power over us so long as we remain steadfast in our faith.

Other epistles in the New Testament also provide us with

Scriptural weapons, including letters from the apostles Peter, James, and Jude. The First Epistle of Peter contains the words of St. Peter, who as the first apostle chosen by Christ and ultimately the Bishop of Rome (and thus the first pope), serves as a potent intercessor in spiritual battles. The letter contains instructions on how to live a Christian life, as well as weapons for times when we face spiritual crises from infernal agents. As he teaches us, "Be alert and of sober mind. Your enemy the devil prowls around like a roaring lion looking for someone to devour. Resist him, standing firm in the faith, because you know that the family of believers throughout the world is undergoing the same kind of sufferings" (1 Peter 5: 8-9). One of the most commanding Scriptural invocations comes to us from the Epistle of James. As one of the Twelve Apostles, James's words carry extreme weight against demonic entities. In his reassurances to the faithful of the fledgling Church, James writes about the power of Christ's name in conflicts against the demonic: "Submit yourselves, then, to God. Resist the devil, and he will flee from you. Father, I surrender all my being to you. I command every satanic oppression to give away and crumble in the mighty name of Jesus." These words come directly from the mouth of James, who was extremely close to Jesus throughout his ministry. His words supply us with yet another source of sacred power to confront the enemies of the spirit.

Prayers

Prayer to the Saints for Spiritual Warfare

The Litany of Saints is one of the most powerful prayers in the canon. Formulated as an invocation, the litany beseeches the most powerful saints to act on our behalf, especially the end of the prayer, which asks for help against Satan and his influence. Although one of the longer prayers in the canon, the Litany maintains a special place because of the sheer volume of saintly intercessors it invokes.

The Litany of Saints:

Lord, have mercy. Lord, have mercy

Christ, have mercy. Christ, have mercy

Lord, have mercy. Lord, have mercy

Christ, hear us. Christ, graciously hear us.

After each response below, the invocation is: Have mercy on us.

God, our heavenly Father,

God the Son, Redeemer of the world,

God the Holy Spirit,

Holy Trinity, one God,

After each response below, the invocation is: Pray for Us

Holy Mary, pray for us.

Holy Mother of God,

Holy Virgin of virgins,

Saint Michael,

Saint Gabriel,

Saint Raphael,

All you holy Angels and Archangels,

All you holy orders of blessed Spirits,

Saint John the Baptist,

Saint Joseph,

All you holy Patriarchs and Prophets,

Saint Peter,

Saint Paul,

Saint Andrew,

Saint James,

Saint John,

Saint Thomas,

Saint James,

Saint Philip,

Saint Bartholomew,

Saint Matthew,

Saint Simon,

Saint Thaddeus,

Saint Matthias,

Saint Barnabas,

Saint Luke,

Saint Mark,

All you holy Apostles and Evangelists,

All you holy Disciples of the Lord,

All you holy Innocents,

Saint Stephen,

Saint Lawrence,

Saint Vincent,

Saint Fabian and Saint Sebastian,

Saint John and Saint Paul,

Saint Cosmas and Saint Damian,

Saint Gervase and Saint Protase,

All you holy Martyrs,

Saint Sylvester,

Saint Gregory,

Saint Ambrose,

Saint Augustine,

Saint Jerome,

Saint Martin,

Saint Nicholas,

All you holy Bishops and Confessors,

All you holy Doctors,

Saint Anthony,

Saint Benedict,

Saint Bernard,

Saint Dominic,

Saint Francis,

All you holy Priests and Clergy,

All you holy Monks and Hermits,

Saint Mary Magdalene,

Saint Agatha,

Saint Lucy,

Saint Agnes,

Saint Cecilia,

Saint Catharine,

Saint Anastasia,

All you holy Virgins and Widows,

All you Saints of God,

After each invocation below, the response is: Lord, save your people

Lord be merciful, Lord save Your people

From every evil,

From every sin,

From Your anger,

From sudden and unforeseen death,

From the snares of the devil,

From anger, hatred, and all ill will,

From the spirit of uncleanness,

From lightening and tempest,

From the scourge of earthquake,

From plague, famine, and war,

From everlasting death,

By the mystery of Your holy Incarnation,

By Your coming,

By Your birth,

By Your baptism and holy fasting,

By Your Cross and suffering,

By Your death and burial,

By Your holy resurrection,

By Your wonderful ascension,

By the coming of the Holy Spirit, the Paraclete,

On the day of Judgment,

After each invocation below, the response is: Lord, hear our prayer.

Be merciful to us sinners, Lord, hear our prayer.

That You will spare us,

That You will pardon us,

That it may please You to bring us to true repentance,

To govern and preserve Your holy Church,

To preserve in holy religion the Pope, and all Holy Orders,

To humble the enemies of holy Church,

To give peace and unity to the whole Christian people,

To recall to the unity of the Church all those who are straying, to bring all unbelievers to the light of the Gospel,

To strengthen and preserve us in Your holy service,

To raise our minds to desire the things of heaven,

To reward all our benefactors with eternal blessings,

To deliver our souls from eternal damnation, and the souls of our brethren, kinsmen, and benefactors,

To give and preserve the fruits of the earth,

To grant eternal rest to all the faithful departed, That it may please You to hear and heed us, Jesus, Son of the living God,

Lamb of God, who takes away the sins of the world,

spare us, O Lord.

Lamb of God, who takes away the sins of the world,

graciously hear us, O Lord.

Lamb of God, who takes away the sins of the world,

have mercy on us.

Christ, hear us. Christ, graciously hear us.

Lord Jesus, hear our prayer. Lord Jesus, hear our prayer.

Lord, have mercy. Lord, have mercy.

Christ, have mercy. Christ, have mercy.

Lord, have mercy. Lord, have mercy.

- Amen.

Invocation of the Heavenly Courts

The Invocation of the Heavenly Courts is a powerful prayer that calls upon the Virgin Mary in her role as Queen of Heaven and foe of Satan. As Eve Redeemed, just as Christ is the Second Adam, the Blessed Mother has great power over evil, "to crush the head of the ancient serpent with thy heel." In doing so, she undoes Satan's treachery in Eden. This prayer also invokes St. Joseph as literal Father of the Universal Church, requesting his aid in repelling evil forces. Lastly, the prayer invokes St. Michael as Satan's fiercest foe, as well as his armies of angels. By calling upon the mightiest members of the Heavenly Court, the

Invocation possesses the authority to protect against demonic influence and proactively repel its advance.

O Glorious Queen of Heaven and earth, Virgin Most Powerful, thou who hast the power to crush the head of the ancient serpent with thy heel, come and exercise this power flowing from the grace of thine Immaculate Conception.

Shield us under the mantle of thy purity and love, draw us into the sweet abode of thy heart and annihilate and render impotent the forces bent on destroying us.

Come Most Sovereign Mistress of the Holy Angels and Mistress of the Most Holy Rosary, thou who from the very beginning hast received from God the power and the mission to crush the head of Satan.

We humbly beseech thee, send forth thy holy legions, that under thy command and by thy power they may pursue the evil spirits, encounter them on every side, resist their bold attacks and drive them far from us, harming no one on the way, binding them immobile to the foot of the Cross to be judged and sentenced by Jesus Christ Thy Son and to be disposed of by Him as He wills.

St Joseph, Patron of the Universal Church, come to our aid in this grave battle against the forces of darkness, repel the attacks of the devil and free your son (daughter) N., from the strong hold the enemy has upon his (her) soul.

St. Michael, summon the entire heavenly court to engage their forces in this fierce battle against the powers of hell.

Come O Prince of Heaven with thy mighty sword and thrust into hell Satan and all the other evil spirits. O Guardian Angels, guide and protect us. Amen.

Prayer of Command

The Prayer of Command is explicit in its purpose to drive out demonic forces through a powerful invocation of Christ. This prayer not only casts out evil influence but also serves to break any negative abjurations such as curses. In addition, this prayer confers protection from further demonic interference, specifically targeting an afflicted person with its grace.

In His name and by the power of His Cross and Blood, I ask Jesus to bind any evil spirits, forces and powers of the earth, air, fire, or water, of the netherworld and the satanic forces of nature.

By the power of the Holy Spirit and by His authority, I ask Jesus Christ to break any curses, hexes, or spells and send them back to where they came from, if it be His Holy Will.

I beseech Thee Lord Jesus to protect us by pouring Thy Precious Blood on us (my family, etc.), which Thou hast shed for us and I ask Thee to command that any departing spirits leave quietly, without disturbance, and go straight to Thy Cross to dispose of as Thou sees fit.

I ask Thee to bind any demonic interaction, interplay or communications.

I place N. (person, place or thing) under the protection of the Blood of Jesus Christ which He shed for us.

- Amen.

Spiritual Warfare Prayer

Also known as The Prayer for Destroying Demonic Influence, this benediction attacks all forms of diabolical interference. Through an invocation of Christ, the prayer requests liberation from the various manifestations of the demonic in our lives. Also, the prayer invokes the angels in their role as soldiers to fight against evil in the world. Intended to be recited in the morning before the start of our day, this prayer is both protective and proactive, granting us the strength to resist temptation while also shielding us from potential threats we may encounter.

Through the power of Lord Jesus Christ of Nazareth, I come against every source of sin in my life. I ask you Lord Jesus to send forth an assignment of warring angels to strike down and destroy every demonic entity that has been influencing my sinful behaviors of envy, criticism, impatience, resentment, pride, rebellion, stubbornness, unforgiveness, gossip, disobedience, strife, violence, divorce, accusation, anger, manipulation, jealousy, greed, laziness, revenge, coveting, possessiveness, control, retaliation, selfishness, deceitfulness, deception, dishonesty, unbelief, seduction, lust, pornography, masturbation, idolatry and witchcraft.

May your warring angels strike down and destroy every demonic influence that has contributed to my physical and psychological infirmities of nerve disorder, lung disorder, brain disorder or dysfunction, AIDS, cancer, hypochondria, hyperactivity, depression, schizophrenia, fatigue, anorexia, bulimia, addictions, gluttony, perfectionism, alcoholism, self-abuse, sexual addictions, sexual perversions, attempted suicide, incest, pedophilia, lesbianism, homosexuality, adultery, homophobia, confusion, ignorance, procrastination, self-hatred, isolation, loneliness, ostracism, paranoia, nervousness, passivity, indecision, doubt, oppression, rejection, poor self-image, anxiety, shame, timidity and fear.

I arise today through the power of the Lord Jesus Christ and ask to be filled with the Holy Spirit's gifts of peace, patience, love, joy, kindness, generosity, faithfulness, gentleness, self-control, humility, forgiveness, goodness, fortitude, discipline, truth, relinquishment, good self-image, prosperity, charity, obedience, a sound mind, order, fulfillment in Christ, acceptance of self, acceptance of others, trust, freedom from addictions, freedom of having-to-control, freedom from shame, wholeness, wellness, health, wisdom, knowledge, understanding, and the light and life of the Lord Jesus Christ. Amen.

Prayer of Protection

The Prayer of Protection is a short, simple, yet powerful benediction. This prayer primarily serves a defensive function as it beseeches Christ's protection against Satan and his minions, specifically citing "clinging, familial, familiar or retaliating spirits." This includes demons responsible for infestation, those vexing a particular family, and other evil forces acting on behalf of the Evil One. One feature of this prayer is its inclusion of signing yourself with either holy water or chrism, which enhance the protective effects of the prayer itself.

I ask Jesus to seal me in His most Precious Blood

against any and all incursions of the evil one,

in particular against any clinging, familial, familiar or retaliating spirits,

in the name of the Father and of the Son and of the Holy Spirit.

- Amen.

(If you have blessed oil or water, sign yourself on the forehead with it at this moment)

Prayer for Protection Against Curses, Harm, Accidents

This prayer specifically addresses the risks posed by curses and the devastation they can cause. Although brief, this simple benediction has the potential to protect us from maledictions and to dispel any that may already be afflicting us. The reversal of curses finds its roots in many Old Testament decrees, such as Genesis 12:3, where God states: "And I will bless them that bless thee, and curse him that curseth thee: and in thee shall all families of the earth be blessed." In the same way, this prayer brings to mind Paul's teaching in his Letter to the Galatians, when he tells us that "Christ redeemed us from the curse of the law by become a curse for us, for it is written: 'Cursed is everyone who is hung on a tree'" (Gal. 3:13-14). When we set our requests at the foot of the Cross, we ask Christ to step on the head of the serpent as he did in the Garden of Gethsemane, just as Michael the Archangel did when he cast Lucifer from Heaven. In its invocation of the angels, this prayer also calls to mind a verse from the Book of Psalms: "He shall cover thee with feathers, and under his wings shalt thou trust: his truth shall be thy shield and buckler" (91:4).

Lord Jesus, I ask Thee to protect my family from sickness, from all harm and from accidents. If any of us has been subjected to any curses, hexes, or spells, I beg Thee to declare these curses, hexes or spells null and void. If any evil spirits have been sent against us, I ask that these evil spirits be sent to the foot of His cross to be dealt with as He wills. Then, Lord, I ask Thee to send Thy holy Angels to guard and protect all of us. Amen.

Prayer for Breaking Curses

Much like the Prayer for Protection Against Curses, this prayer is one of deliverance, unbinding any curses affecting us or our loved ones. This prayer is also unique in its focus on divine justice, placing as it does a sort of counter-curse at its conclusion, returning curses back upon those that cast them, as we noted in God's promise in Genesis 12:3 to curse those who curse us.

In the name of Jesus Christ, I now rebuke, break, and loose myself and my family from any and all evil curses, fetishes, charms, vexes, hexes, spells, every jinx, all psychic powers, sorcery, bewitchments, enchantments, witchcraft, love potions, and psychic prayers that have been put upon me, back to ten generations on both sides of my family. I break and loose myself from any and all connected or related spirits from any person or persons or from any occult or psychic sources. I ask You, Heavenly Father, to return them to the senders now. Let him that loves cursing receive it unto himself.

An alternative version from the Catechism reads as follows:

In the name of the Lord Jesus Christ of Nazareth, by the power of his cross, his blood and his resurrection, I take authority over all curses, hexes, spells, voodoo practices, witchcraft assignments, satanic rituals, incantations and evil wishes that have been sent my way, or have passed down the generational bloodline. I break their influence over my life by the power of the risen Lord Jesus Christ, and I command these curses to go back to where they came from and be replaced with a blessing.

I ask forgiveness for and denounce all negative inner vows and agreements that I have made with the enemy, and I ask that you Lord Jesus Christ release me from any bondage they may have held in me. I claim your shed blood over all aspects of my life, relationships, ministry endeavors and finances. I thank you for your enduring love, your angelic protection, and for the fullness of your abundant blessings.

Prayer for Breaking Occult Ties

This prayer follows a formula similar to the benediction proclaimed during the Sacrament of Baptism and later in the Sacrament of Confirmation. By denouncing "Satan and all his works," we profess our allegiance to the Light and our rejection of Darkness. Invoking all three members of the Holy Trinity, this prayer musters all the might of the Divine to dispel any negative traces brought on by dabbling with dark magic or Satanic forces. Here we should again note that some of the practices mentioned in this prayer are not *de facto* evil but only risk spiritual corruption when practiced through malevolent powers or spirits opposed to the Divine. As we've discussed in passing before, the use of white magic in certain witch practices is not affected by this prayer, nor is the use of mediums as long as they draw their power from a sacred source untainted by demonic influence.

Heavenly Father, in the name of your only begotten Son, Jesus Christ, I renounce Satan and all his works, all forms of witchcraft, the use of divination, the practice of sorcery, dealing with mediums, channeling with spirit guides, the Ouija board, astrology, Reiki, hypnosis, automatic writing, horoscopes, numerology, all types of fortune telling, palm readings, levitation, and anything else associated with the occult or Satan. I denounce all of them in the name of Jesus Christ who came in the flesh, and by the power of his cross, his blood and his resurrection, I break their hold over my life.

I confess all these sins before you and ask you to cleanse and forgive me. I ask you Lord Jesus to enter my heart and create in me the kind of person you have intended me to be. I ask you to send forth the gifts of your Holy Spirit to baptize me, just as you baptized your disciples on the day of Pentecost.

I thank you heavenly Father for strengthening my inner spirit with the power of your Holy Spirit, so that Christ may dwell in my heart. Through faith, rooted and grounded in love, may I be able to comprehend with all the saints, the breadth, length, height and depth of Christ's love which surpasses all knowledge. Amen.

Prayer for Psychic Heredity and Breaking Bondage*

Specifically intended for breaking generational curses, this deliverance prayer casts a wide net of blessings, covering not only the supplicant but also their entire extended family. Since generational curses afflict entire families, this prayer serves to dispel such curses while also offering continued protection against future evil intent.

In the name of Jesus, I now renounce, break, free, and loose myself and my family from all psychic heredity, demonic holds, psychic powers, and bondage of physical and mental illnesses, family, marital, and other curses upon us, back to ten generations on both sides of our families resulting from sins, transgressions, iniquities, occult and psychic involvements of myself, my parents, and any other ancestors of mine or my spouse, and all ex-spouses, or their parents, or any of their ancestors. I plead the blood of Jesus, in the Name of Jesus declaring that the enemy cannot penetrate the blood of Jesus.

Prayer Against Every Evil Eye

The evil eye, or "malochia," is found in nearly every cultural tradition. Although technically a curse, the evil eye is most frequently cast without intent, a fundamental aspect of curses in general. The prayer for protection against the Evil Eye included below is one adapted from the Orthodox tradition.

O Lord our God, King of the ages, the almighty and all-powerful, who by thy will alone dost create and transform all things; who didst transform the sevenfold furnace and the flame of Babylon into dew and didst preserve thy Three Holy Youths safe; thou who art the physician and healer of our souls; the safekeeping of all those that hope in thee; we pray to thee and beseech thee, banish, expel and cast away every diabolical action, every satanic attack and every plot, every evil curiosity and harm and spell of the evil eye caused by malicious and evil people from thy servant [insert name here]; and if this has occurred because of beauty, or bravery, or prosperity, or jealousy and envy, or the evil eye, do thou O Master and Lover of mankind, stretch forth thy mighty hand and thy strong arm from on high and keep watch over this thy creature and send down upon him/her an angel of peace, a mighty guardian of soul and body, who will rebuke and banish from him/her every wicked intention, every sorcery and the evil eye of destructive and envious men; so that being guarded by thee, thy supplicant may sing to thee with thanksgiving: The Lord is my helper, and I shall not be afraid, what can man do unto me? And again: I shall fear no evil for thou art with me. For thou art God, my strength, the mighty counsellor, the Prince of peace, the Father of the age to come. Yea, O Lord our God, spare thy creature and save thy servant from every harm and influence brought about by the evil eye, and preserve him/her safe above every evil. Through the intercessions of the Mother of God and ever Virgin Mary, of the luminous Archangels and of all thy saints. Amen.

An alternative version of the prayer against the Evil Eye is an invocation directly to Mary, known as Consecration to Mary for the Closing of the "Occult Third Eye"[62] This prayer is intended for use by the afflicted themselves. Not only does the prayer offer protection from the Evil Eye, but also aims at cleansing already existing demonic interference. This version is most appropriate for use by those who feel their studies in the occult have somehow invited negative energy into their lives.

O Most Immaculate and Loving Virgin Mary, Mother of God and My Mother, who was present in the crucifixion and death of your Son Jesus on the hill of Calvary, have mercy on me, your son (your daughter). Have mercy on this poor, suffering body of mine harassed and suppressed by the Evil one. Through the merits of your sorrows, grant me relief and comfort. Close

---

[62] Syquia, Handbook of Deliverance Prayers, p. 204

now my psychic abilities which I have obtained through the power of demons. These psychic abilities I denounce and surrender totally to you. I consecrate myself to you. I offer myself to you. Hear my supplications, dearest Mother and Queen. Through the love you have for your Son Jesus who has entrusted me to your maternal care. Amen.

Prayer of Deliverance

Deliverance prayers make up an entire body of benedictions, but the official Prayer of Deliverance from the Catechism offers strong protection through its invocation of the most powerful archangels—Michael, Raphael, and Gabriel—and the host of saints. Much like the Litany of Saints, this prayer benefits from the powerful intercessors involved, but unlike the Litany, it specifically targets the demonic interferences related directly to sin. The list of sins and negative influences listed in the prayer are more comprehensive than merely the Seven Deadly Sins, but the intent is the same: liberation from sin and temptation in order to cleanse the spirit and start anew.

My Lord, You are all powerful. You are God, the Father.

We beg You through the intercession and help of the archangels

Michael, Raphael, and Gabriel

For the deliverance of our brothers and sisters

Who are enslaved by the evil one.

All saints of heaven come to our aid:

From anxiety, sadness, and obsessions, We beg You, Free us, O Lord

From hatred, fornication, envy, We beg You, Free us, O Lord

From thoughts of jealousy, rage, and death, We beg You, Free us, O Lord

From every thought of suicide and abortion, We beg You, Free us, O Lord

From every form of sinful sexuality, We beg You, Free us, O Lord

From every division in our family, and every harmful friendship, We beg You, Free us, O Lord

From every sort of spell, malefice, witchcraft, and form of occult, We be You, Free us, O Lord

Lord, You who said, "I leave you peace, my peace I give to you,"

Grant that through the intercession of the Virgin may [I/we] may be liberated

From every evil spell and enjoy your love always

In the Name of Christ, Our Lord,

- Amen

Prayer for Troubled Souls*

Most prayers for troubled souls involve praying for the deceased who may be in Purgatory. These prayers are intended to expedite the purification process and ensure these souls' transition to Paradise. The most famous scriptural reference, among others, concerning these prayers comes from the Old Testament, where we read that "a holy and wholesome thought to pray for the dead, that they may be loosed from sins" (2 Maccabees 12:46).

A standard prayer for souls in Purgatory, The Prayer for the Most Forgotten Soul, goes thus:

O Lord God Almighty,

I beseech Thee by the Precious

Body and Blood of Thy Divine Son Jesus,

which He Himself on the night before His Passion

gave as meat and drink to His beloved Apostles

and bequeathed to His Holy Church

to be the perpetual Sacrifice

and life-giving nourishment of His faithful people,

deliver the souls in purgatory,

but most of all,

that soul which was most devoted

to this Mystery of infinite love,

in order that it may praise Thee therefore,

together with Thy Divine Son

and the Holy Spirit in Thy glory for ever.

- Amen.

The Franciscan Order has prayers intended to aid souls facing trouble in their lives. These prayers follow a more liturgical structure, combining invocations with passages from Scripture and are intended to be recited at a gathering of the faithful. One Franciscan prayer for troubled souls among the living reads as follows:

In Times of Trouble

Opening Prayer

Jesus said, "Do not let your hearts be troubled. Have faith in God and faith in me " And so we begin in the name of the Father, and of the Son, and of the Holy Spirit.

Scripture

If God is for us, who is against us? He who did not withhold his own Son, but gave him up for all of us, will he not with him also give us everything else? (Romans 8:31–32)

Petitions

Response: We trust you, Lord. Show us your mercy and love, we pray...

Help us in these difficult times, we pray...

Stay with us in these troubled times, we pray...

Add your own petitions.

Collective

Our hearts are restless, O Lord, until they rest in you.

Prayer Against Oppression

This prayer is actually a formal part of the Rite of Minor

Exorcism, which may be performed by laity.[63] After the imprecatory formula where the supplicant reclaims control of their life through their faith to the Trinity, an imperative formula follows: "I bind all demons of oppression . . . and I command you to leave and go to the foot of the Holy Cross to receive your sentence..." This formula casts the evil spirit out by invoking the mightiest spiritual intercessors: Christ, the Blessed Mother, St. Michael, St. Peter, St. Paul, and the legion of saints and angels.

Most Blessed Trinity, by the authority given to me by the natural law and by Thy giving these things & rights to me, I claim authority, rights and power over my N. (income, finances, possessions, etc.) and anything else that pertains to the oppression. By the merits of Thy Sacred Wounds, I reclaim the rights, powers and authority over anything which I may have lost or conceded to any demon and I ask Thee to remove any demon's ability to influence or affect anything in my life. God the Father humiliate the demons that have sought to steal Thy glory from Thee by oppressing Thy creatures. We beseech Thee to show Thy great glory and power over them and Thy great generosity to me, Thine unworthy creature, by answering all that I have asked of Thee. I bind all demons of oppression, in the name of Jesus, by the power of the Most Precious Blood, the power of the humility with which Christ suffered His wounds, and the intercession of the Blessed Virgin Mary, Virgin Most Powerful, Saint Michael the Archangel, the blessed Apostles, Peter and Paul, and all the saints, and I command you to leave and go to the foot of the Holy Cross to receive your sentence, in the

---

[63] Ripperger, Laity, p. 43

Name of the Father, and of the Son and of the Holy Spirit. Amen.

Prayer to be Freed of Evil Habits

Also known as the First Prayer of Renunciation, this benediction adapts itself to the evil habit in question. Closely related to ties for breaking occult ties, this prayer is also a type of deliverance prayer, the supplicant asking to be freed from a particular negative influence in their lives. The prayer begins much like the formulas used in the sacraments of Baptism, Penance, and Confirmation. This prayer acts in conjunction with Reconciliation when we confess our sins to Christ through the confessor *in persona Christi*. The result is immense. "When God forgives a sinner who humbly confesses his sin," St. Bernard of Clairvaux once stated, "the devil loses his dominion over the heart he had taken." When we undertake penance and renounce temptation and evil deeds, we repel Satan and his influence from our lives.

In the Name of Jesus, I renounce Satan, all dealings with the occult, all action of Satan on my spirit, my soul, and my body, and all connections with his servants.

I renounce in particular the Spirit:

Of Superstition, of Disobedience, of Anger, of Sacrilege, of Division, of Violence, of Curse, of Family Discord, of Vengeance, of Malediction, of

Weakness, of Hatred, of Blasphemy, of Injustice, of Rancor, of Pride, of Untruthfulness, of Refusal to forgive, of Haughtiness, of Dissimulation, of Spitefulness, of Domination, of Hypocrisy, of Stinginess, of Vanity, of Curiosity, of Covetousness, of Contempt, of Scandal, of Envy, of Agitation, of Calumny, of Jealousy, of Confusion, of Criticism, of Intemperance, of Depression, of Indiscretion, of Alcoholism, of Fear, of Gossip, of Drug Addiction, of Anguish, of Laziness, of Despair, of Suicide, of Fornication, of Sorcery, of Folly, of Adultery, of Evil Spells, of Rebellion, of Irritation, of Deviation...

And all other Spirits of Destruction such as:

The Spirit that hinders prayer, the Spirit causing sleeplessness, the Spirit causing aversion to study, the Spirit provoking illnesses, the Spirit exacerbating illnesses, the Spirits afflicting my body. [Additional afflictions can be inserted here]

- Amen.

Prayer to Saint Michael the Archangel

Attributed to Pope Leo XIII in the late 19th century, this prayer has a fascinating history. Leo experienced a vision that Satan would come to earth and wreak great destruction in the 20th century. Many commentators have noted the horrors of the World Wars as evidence of Leo's vision. The prayer is especially powerful because, during the war in Heaven, it was St. Michael the Archangel, the leader of God's armies, who cast Satan out of Heaven into the pits of Hell. According to Revelation, he will once again lead the forces of good against the Anti-Christ on the Fields of Megiddo.

Visions of St. Michael go back all the way to the first on Monte Gargano in fifth-century Italy. Afterwards, in the eighth century, Michael appeared to St. Aubert at the site of the Abbey of Mont-Saint-Michel in Normandy, one of the most important sites in Europe. As the patron saint of soldiers, Michael functions as a powerful intercessor in both physical and spiritual combat. He is also the patron saint of grocers, radiologists, and police officers; thus, those involved in those professions gain additional benefits from invoking him in God's name. The prayer goes as follows:

Saint Michael the Archangel, defend us in battle.

Be our defense against the wickedness and snares of the Devil.

May God rebuke him, we humbly pray,

and do thou, O Prince of the heavenly hosts,

by the power of God,

thrust into hell Satan, and all the evil spirits,

who prowl about the world

seeking the ruin of souls.

- Amen.

Prayers to Other Holy Angels

The Prayer to Holy Angels stems back to the medieval Church tradition, where the hierarchy of angels was established as an orderly system of benevolent spirits based on their closeness to God. References to the higher orders of angels—Thrones, Denominations, Principalities, etc.—might initially seem unfamiliar to those who have not studied angelology, but they follow a long spiritual tradition. The ordering here follows Psellus and others, who place angels at the lowest tier and Seraphim as the most powerful angels.

This prayer takes special care to invoke our personal Guardian Angel, a tradition with Scriptural roots that gained popularity in the Middle Ages. In recent years, interest in Guardian Angels has only continued to grow, and they remain a powerful source of spiritual protection. As St. John Vianney once said about the role of guardian angels in our spiritual battles, "If only we could see the joy of our guardian angel when he sees us fighting our temptations!" Similarly, St. John Bosco instructs us that "When tempted, invoke your Angel. He is more eager to help you than you are to be helped! Ignore the devil, and do not be afraid of him: He trembles and flees at the sight of your Guardian Angel."

Angels of all ranks, from the highest Seraphim to our own personal Guardians, can come to our aid in times of spiritual crisis.

Bless the Lord, All you His Angels, You who are Mighty in strength And do His Will.

Intercede for me At the throne of God, And by your unceasing watchfulness Protect me in every danger Of soul and body.

Bless the Lord, All you His Angels, You who are Mighty in strength And do His Will.

Intercede for me At the throne of God, And by your unceasing watchfulness Protect me in every danger Of soul and body.

Obtain for me The grace of final perseverance, So that after this life I may be admitted To your glorious company And may sing with you The praises of God For all eternity.

O all you holy Angels And Archangels, Thrones and Dominations, Principalities and Powers And Virtues of heaven, Cherubim and Seraphim And especially you, My dear Guardian Angel, Intercede for me And obtain for me The special favor I now ask.

(State your intention here...).

[*The prayer recommends saying 9 Our Fathers at the end, once for each of the Angelic Orders. This form of repetition, much like the tradition of the Rosary, acts as a mantra and helps promote meditation through prayer.]

Prayer to Overcome Evil Spirits and Enemies

Also known as the Prayer to Bind and Blind Demons, this benediction provides a mighty weapon against the diabolical. Through direct invocations of the Blessed Mother and Christ, the prayer is a form of aggressive prayer, attacking the demonic entity and protecting the supplicant from demonic retaliation. By blinding demons to our actions, we can prevent them from causing us further harm and better protect ourselves and our households from their negative influence.

Most gracious Virgin Mary, thou who wouldst crush the head of the serpent, protect us from the vengeance of the evil one.

We offer our prayers, supplications, sufferings and good works to you so that you may purify them, sanctify them and present them to thy Son as a perfect offering.

May this offering be given so that the demons that influence us (could influence us or name the person) do not know the source of the expulsion and blindness.

Blind them so they know not our good works.

Blind them so that they know not on whom to take vengeance.

Blind them so that they may receive the just sentence for their works.

Cover us with the Precious Blood of thy Son so that we may enjoy the protection which flows from His Passion and Death.

We ask this through the same Christ Our Lord.

- Amen.

Prayer for Healing

This prayer addresses physical healing. Although many such prayers exist, the Catechism provides a variety that targets specific illnesses and ailments. This particular prayer asks for healing of the body in general.

Lord Jesus, through that faith which You gave to me at Baptism, I worship You and thank You. You are the Son of God who became man. You are the Messiah, the Savior. At this moment I way to say to You as Peter did: there is no other name under heaven given to men by which we are to be saved. I accept you, Lord Jesus, in my heart and in my life; I want You to take absolute lordship over my life. Forgive me my sins just like you forgave the sins of the paralytic in the Gospel. Cleanse me with Your divine Blood!

I lay down at your feet all my sufferings and infirmities.

Heal me, Lord, by the power of Your glorified Wounds, by the power of Your Cross and Most Precious Blood! You are the Good Shepherd and I am but one of the sheep from our flock: Take pity on me!

Jesus, You are the One who said: ask and it will be given to you. The people from Galilee brought their sick before You and You healed them. You never change. Your power is the line. I believe that You can heal me for You have the same compassion for me that You felt towards the sick whom you cured because You are the Resurrection and the Life. Thank You, Jesus, for what You will do for me.

I accept the plan of Your Love for me. I believe that You will reveal Your glory to me. Before even knowing how You will come to my aid, I praise You and thank You.

- Amen.

Prayer for Inner Healing

Several prayers are officially recognized in the Catechism for inner healing. However, the most common one is perhaps most relevant today. Not only does this prayer address inner turmoil in general, but also directly addresses one of the most intrusive issues in our daily lives: anxiety. Although anxiety often stems from psychological causes, oftentimes, it is a symptom of spiritual disturbance.

Lord Jesus, You came to heal our wounded and troubled hearts. I beg You to heal the torments that cause anxiety in my heart; I beg You, in a particular way, to heal all who are the cause of sin. I beg You to come into my life and heal me of the psychological harms that struck me in my early years and form the injuries that they caused throughout my life. Lord Jesus, You know my burdens. I lay them all on Your Good Shepherd's Heart. I beseech You -- by the merits of the great, open wound in Your heart -- to heal the small wounds that are in mine. Heal the pain of my memories, so that nothing that has happened to me will cause me to remain in pain and anguish, filled with anxiety.

Another prayer from the Catechism addressing inner healing reads as follows:

Heal, O Lord, all those wounds that have been the cause of all the evil that is rooted in my life. I want to forgive all those who have offended me. Look to those inner sores that make me unable to forgive. You Who came to forgive the afflicted of heart, please, heal my own heart.

Heal, my Lord Jesus, those intimate wounds that cause me physical illness. I offer You my heart. Accept it, Lord, purify it, and give me the sentiments of Your Divine Heart. Help me to be meek and humble.

Heal me, O Lord, from the pain caused by the death of my loved ones, which is oppressing me. Grant me to regain peace and joy in the knowledge that You are the Resurrection and the Life. Make me an authentic witness to Your Resurrection, Your victory over sin and death, Your living presence among us.

- Amen.

Prayer for Purification

The Prayer for Purification has a long history, dating back to the earliest days of the Church. Much like invocations asking for the Armor of God, the Prayer of Purification is both shield and sword. The imagery is especially striking in the last verse, where the Armor is compared to the Veil of the Blessed Mother and a briar from the Crown of Thorns. More than mere metaphors, these images represent the literal protective powers granted by the spirits being invoked.

Jesus, pour Thy Precious Blood over me, my body, mind, soul, and spirit; my conscious and subconscious; my intellect and will; my feelings, thoughts, emotions and passions; my words and actions; my vocation, my relationships, family, friends and possessions. Protect with Thy Precious Blood all other activities of my life. Lord I dedicate all of these things to Thee, and I acknowledge Thee as Lord and Master of all.

Mary, Immaculate Conception, pure and holy Virgin Mother of Our Lord Jesus Christ, draw each of us under Thy veil; guard me and shield me against all attacks and temptations that would violate the virtue of chastity.

Lord Jesus Christ, I beg Thee for the grace to remain guarded beneath the protective mantle of Mary, surrounded by the holy briar from which was taken the Holy Crown of Thorns, and saturated with Thy Precious Blood in the power of the Holy Spirit, with our Guardian Angels for the greater glory of the Father.

- Amen.

Prayers for Strength

Many prayers for strength exist in the Apostolic tradition. The Prayer to St. Gabriel for Strength remains one of the most effective, drawing upon the archangel's power as the messenger of God for strength against the powers of darkness. As one of God's principle warriors, armed with the Spear and Shield of the Almighty, Gabriel stands as one of Satan's greatest foes. As the one who proclaimed to the Blessed Mother the impending arrival of the Son of God, Gabriel is also the mouthpiece of the Lord, reinforcing our spirits just as he reinforced Mary's in her initial disbelief. Gabriel's close relationship with Mary further bolsters his status as a supreme opponent of Satan and his armies.

O Gabriel, might of God, who announced to the Virgin Mary the incarnation of the only Son of God, and in the garden consoled and strengthen Christ oppressed with fear and sorrow; I give honor to you, O chosen spirit, and humbly pray to you to be my advocate with Jesus Christ my Savior, and with Mary His Blessed Virgin Mother; in all my trials assist me, lest I be overcome by temptation and may I give praise and thanksgiving to my God in all things. - Amen.

Perhaps the prayer most familiar across traditions is The Prayer for Strength, which is intended as a daily recitation in the morning. One benefit of this invocation is its protective properties, summoning God as your shield against both earthly and unearthly challenges.

Lord God, I pray to You with utmost humility that You give me strength as I carry my cross today. There are so many challenges in my life that are draining my strength. When I am too weak, carry me, when I am tired, give me rest, when I fall, lift me up, when I am hungry feed me and when I am thirsty, quench me.

Almighty God, I know You are my Protection, my strength, my Shield, and my defender. I pray that You be at my side for I do not know who or what I will come across today.

Please help me to attach myself to You today. Also, teach me how to stand strong in You and choose only Your way on this day. Help me walk in Your truth and not my feelings.

Lord help me embrace anything that comes my way as a chance to see You at work and as an opportunity to point others Your way. Father, thank You for loving me and nothing can ever take that away from me! Amen.

Another common prayer for strength works best during times of personal weakness, a time which St. John Paul II reminds us is when Satan is most likely to strike.

O living Temple of the divinity, my heart is in darkness, and in you the fullness of wisdom inhabits corporally—my heart is weak, yours is the throne of omnipotence-my heart is fearful and afflicted, oppressed, and craving after happiness, but despairing to find it; in you alone, and in imitating you is my true happiness to be sought, and in you for the future I will seek it.

Grant me the strength I need and may I always turn to your Divine Heart in my times of trial.

- Amen.

A more recent prayer is one by St. John Paul II himself, who devised this prayer invoking St. Padre Pio when he canonized him. The prayer asks for strength during times of suffering:[64]

Teach us, we ask you, humility of heart so we may be counted among the little ones of the Gospel, to whom the Father promised to reveal the mysteries of his Kingdom. Help us to pray without ceasing, certain that God knows what we need even before we ask him. Obtain for us the eyes of faith that will be able to recognize right away in the poor and suffering the face of Jesus. Sustain us in the hour of the combat and of the trial and, if we fall, make us experience the joy of the sacrament of forgiveness. Grant us your tender devotion to Mary, the Mother of Jesus and our Mother. Accompany us on our earthly pilgrimage toward the blessed homeland, where we hope to arrive in order to contemplate forever the glory of the Father, the Son and the Holy Spirit. Amen.

---

[64] https://aleteia.org/2020/09/23/john-paul-iis-prayer-to-st-padre-pio-for-strength-during-suffering/

PART 5

Maintaining Victory

Once we've achieved victory in a spiritual battle, we must then maintain it. How do we accomplish this? How do we protect ourselves, our loved ones, and our homes from further demonic intrusions? We have already investigated ways to prevent satanic interference, strategies for confronting demonic entities, and practices from the tradition that supply us with additional defenses. However, maintaining victory means remaining vigilant, sustaining our faith in both belief and practice, and arming ourselves with the tools necessary for keeping Satan and his agents at bay.

Vigilance is vital to maintaining victory because, all too often, after we win a spiritual battle, we grow complacent. As St. Peter tells us, "Be alert and of sober mind. Your enemy, the devil, prowls around like a roaring lion looking for someone to devour. Resist him, standing firm in the faith, because you know that the family of believers throughout the world is undergoing the same kind of sufferings" (1 Peter 5: 8-9). We must remember that no victory over Satan or his forces, no matter how great or small, is ever permanent. The Evil One never relents in his quest to corrupt us and sow doubt in our lives, so we must never relent in our awareness of this threat. As soon as we let down our guard, our victory is threatened. We must continue to wear the Armor of God, but we must also keep His sword at our side at all times.

Our primary weapons in this regard are similar to those we explored in previous sections, except these are aimed at increasing our vigilance, heightening our spiritual connection with the Divine to reinforce our Armor, and deploying any and all tools at our disposal to crush the Serpent before he has a chance to strike us again. These weapons include prayers designed specifically for protection, sacred objects and relics to sanctify us and the space around us, and ritual practices such as reciting the rosary, fortifying our faith, and strengthening our spirit.

Vigilance implies focus. One of the primary ways to achieve maximum levels of vigilance is through practiced contemplation. Contemplation involves more than mere meditation. As Mother Teresa reminds us, "Seeking the face of God in everything, everyone, everywhere, all the time, and seeing His hand in every happening—that is contemplation in the heart of the world."[65] By opening our perception to the

---

[65] *In the Heart of the World: Thoughts, Stories, and Prayers* outlines many of Mother Teresa's reflections on suffering and piety.

Divine in the everyday, we move closer to His grace and reinforce the pathways between us and the eternal. In many ways, contemplation is a form of focused meditation. Whereas meditation ultimately aims for us to find unity with Oneness through abandoning ourselves to something greater, contemplation involves heightening our senses to become more fully aware of the omnipresence of the Sacred. Meditation can, of course, come in the form of prayer, to which we turn next.

Prayers

Protection prayers provide the first line of defense. However, the core of the benedictive canon is a necessary prerequisite for all other prayers in our arsenal. These include many familiar to those outside the faith and across Christian traditions, such as the Our Father and the Hail Mary, but also include ancient prayers used in the Liturgy and related practices such as the Mysteries of the Rosary and the Novena. We have already seen that deliverance prayers can dispel demonic interferences, that invoking saintly and angelic intercessors casts out evil from our lives, and that the Word of Scripture embodies divine power. Like our spiritual warfare prayers, the following prayers can be used in confrontations with demonic entities, but they are also used in daily prayer, during the Mass, and to extend the protection granted by successfully dispelling negative interference. These prayers form the core of the Catholic prayerbook and are a necessary component in any complete spiritual arsenal.

The Apostle's Creed

A staple of the catechism, the *Apostle's Creed* has a long history. An important line in the prayer notes that Christ "descended into Hell," a reference to the Harrowing of Hell when, between the Crucifixion and the Resurrection, Christ stormed the Gates of Hell and asserted his everlasting dominance over Satan and the forces of evil. The *Apostle's Creed* is closely related to the *Nicene Creed*,[66] which is recited during Mass before the Holy Sacrament of the Eucharist. In both creeds, we find the fundamental tenets of the Faith. As an expression of belief, the creeds also provide us with a means of reasserting our faith. In situations of spiritual warfare, both the *Apostle's Creed* and the *Nicene Creed* equip us with an affirmation of our allegiance to the Light and our rejection of Satan.

The Apostle's Creed

I believe in God,

the Father Almighty,

---

[66] Burn, A. E. (1909). *The Nicene creed*. London: Rivingtons

Creator of Heaven and earth;

and in Jesus Christ, His only Son, Our Lord,

Who was conceived by the Holy Spirit,

born of the Virgin Mary,

suffered under Pontius Pilate,

was crucified, died, and was buried.

He descended into Hell.

The third day He arose again from the dead;

He ascended into Heaven,

sitteth at the right hand of God, the Father Almighty;

from thence He shall come to judge the living and the dead.

I believe in the Holy Spirit,

the holy Catholic Church,

the communion of saints,

the forgiveness of sins,

the resurrection of the body,

and the life everlasting.

- Amen.

Glory Be

The *Glory Be* prayer is a short summary of the fundamental Catholic beliefs, as well as a supplication to the Trinity and a show of faith in the eternal goodness of the Divine. Although brief, the *Glory Be* can be used in spiritual warfare to great effect. The most potent use of the prayer is in combination with the Holy Rosary, where the *Glory Be* is recited before proceeding through the decades (or sections of ten beads) of the rosary itself.

Glory be to the Father,

and to the Son,

and to the Holy Spirit,

as it was in the beginning,

is now, and ever shall be,

world without end.

- Amen.

Our Father

The *Our Father* holds a special place in the canon of prayers. Recited by virtually every Christian denomination, the Lord's Prayer comes directly from the Gospels, recited at Christ's celebrated Sermon on the Mount. The *Our Father* occupies a central place in our prayer book. Recited at every Mass, this invocation of the Divine is one of the most cherished benedictions in the Tradition because it finds its source in Christ himself. In addition, when recited during Mass, the *Our Father* brings the entire congregation in unison with each other, enhancing the blessedness of the words and their sanctifying effects. Many Catholics and other Christians pray the *Our Father* as part of their daily meditations, another practice that helps us maintain victory against those evil forces waging war against us in our everyday lives.

Our Father,

who art in heaven,

hallowed be thy name;

thy kingdom come;

thy will be done

on earth as it is in heaven.

Give us this day our daily bread;

and forgive us our trespasses

as we forgive those who trespass against us;

and lead us not into temptation,

but deliver us from evil.

- Amen.

Hail Mary

One of the most beloved prayers in the catechism, the *Hail Mary* remains a staple of both daily meditation, special occasions such as births and funerals, and in the various protective and offensive prayer practices in spiritual warfare. The first part of the *Hail Mary* comes from Scripture, combining words from The Annunciation as well as words from the Visitation, when Mary's cousin Elizabeth (mother of John the Baptist) exclaims "Most blessed are you among women, and blessed is the fruit of your womb" upon feeling the Holy Spirit stir Jesus in the womb (Luke 1:42). The second part of the prayer was added by St. Pius V[67] in 1568, a supplication to the Queen of Heaven to absolve of us sins through the power of the Son, and to comfort

---

[67] *Historia Ecclesiasticum.* The original addition by Pius V is found in the Roman Brevary (1598), although earlier versions of this part of the prayer are known from medieval texts in the 14th century.

us when we face our final moments.

Hail Mary, full of grace,

the Lord is with thee[68].

Blessed art thou amongst[69] *women,*

and blessed is the fruit of thy[70] *womb, Jesus.*

Holy Mary, Mother of God,

pray for us sinners,

now and at the hour of our death.

- Amen.

The Angelus

An expanded prayer formula incorporating the *Hail Mary*, the Angelus became a common prayer practice in the Middle Ages, when it was recited at dawn, noon, and dusk. The Angelus recalls the events of the Annunciation when the Archangel Gabriel told the Virgin Mary that she had been chosen to bear the Son of God (Luke 1:26-38). God's choice was determined

---

[68] "you" in the modern version.
[69] "Are you among" in the modern version.
[70] "your"

by both Mary's humble piety and the Immaculate Conception, a core belief in the Church. This principle states that Mary was conceived free of original sin so that Jesus was born as the Second Adam, sent to undo the Original Sin of Eden. The Immaculate Conception is one of the primary reasons the Blessed Mother serves as such a powerful foe of Satan: she remained free of even Satan's first attempt to corrupt humanity.

The prayer also calls us to remember the opening of the Gospel of John, which reveals the Mystery of the Incarnation: "And the Word was made flesh, and dwelt among us" (1:14). When we pray to the Angelus, we are embracing the sacred mysteries of Christ becoming the human embodiment of God's divine Word. Since the coming of Christ represents Satan's ultimate humiliation, the Angelus protects against demonic interference by invoking the defeat of the Evil One at the hands of the Son of God. More importantly, the prayer is designed to be recited by two people, encouraging us toward spiritual practice as a community rather than alone. As participants in a grand tradition, we are never far from our fellows in faith.

V - The Angel of the Lord declared unto Mary.

R - And she conceived by the Holy Spirit.

(Recite Hail Mary....)

V - Behold the handmaid of the Lord.

R - Be it done unto me according to thy word.

(Recite Hail Mary....)

V- And the Word was made Flesh.

R- And dwelt among us.

(Recite Hail Mary....)

V- Pray for us, O Holy Mother of God.

R- That we may be made worthy of the promises of Christ.

LET US PRAY: Pour forth, we beseech Thee, O Lord, Thy grace into our hearts; that, we to whom the Incarnation of Christ, Thy Son, was made known by the message of an Angel, may by His Passion and Cross, be brought to the glory of His Resurrection through the same Christ our Lord. Amen.

Prayer to St. Joseph

As the husband of the Blessed Mother and the man who raised Jesus, St. Joseph occupies a special place in the canon of saints. As the patron of the Universal Church (recall "catholic" means "universal" in Greek), Joseph also acts as a fatherly figure for all faithful, a protector and advisor who instructed Jesus in his earthly life in the virtues of diligence, honesty, and faith. The Prayer to St. Joseph was written in 1889 by Pope Leo XIII and added to the canonical rosary ritual after his encyclical

Quamquam pluries was published. The prayer is both an intercessory and a protective measure, asking for Joseph's protection in his role as the earthly father of Christ.

Prayer to Saint Joseph:

To you, O blessed Joseph,

do we come in our tribulation?

and having implored the help of your most holy Spouse,

we confidently invoke your patronage also.

Through that charity which bound you

to the Immaculate Virgin Mother of God

and through the paternal love

with which you embraced the Child Jesus,

we humbly beg you graciously to regard the inheritance

which Jesus Christ has purchased by his Blood,

and with your power and strength to aid us in our necessities.

O most watchful guardian of the Holy Family,

defend the chosen children of Jesus Christ;

O most loving father, ward off from us

every contagion of error and corrupting influence;

O our most mighty protector, be kind to us

and from heaven assist us in our struggle

with the power of darkness.

As once you rescued the Child Jesus from deadly peril,

so now protect God's Holy Church

from the snares of the enemy and from all adversity;

shield, too, each one of us by your constant protection,

so that, supported by your example and your aid,

we may be able to live piously, to die in holiness,

and to obtain eternal happiness in heaven.

- Amen.

The Act of Contrition

The *Act of Contrition* is an integral part of the Sacrament of Reconciliation, also known as penance or contrition. This sacrament is a ritual intended to restore the grace imparted upon the faithful at Baptism, cleansing the soul of any sins and asking for protection against the temptation to sin again. Confessing our sins to a priest acting *in persona Christi* unburdens our souls from the weight of our misdeeds. Importantly, we must remember to be honest in our confession. As St. Margaret of Cortona once put it, "Hide nothing from your confessor...a sick man can only be cured by revealing his wounds." When we confess, we bare our souls before Christ and humbly ask his forgiveness.

In addition, confession prepares us to receive the Eucharist because to do so we must be pure of spirit. When we ask forgiveness, we also participate in consolation by purifying our hearts. As we are reminded in the Beatitudes, those pure of heart are specially blessed by God, granting them a privileged place through a state of grace.

O my God, I am heartfully sorry for having offended thee,

and I detest all my sins because of Thy just punishment,

but most of all because I have offended Thee my Lord,

Who is all good and deserving of all my love.

I firmly resolve, with the help of Thy grace, to sin no more,

and to avoid the near occasion of sin.

Amen.

The Novena

Novenas are in many respects similar to the rosary as a combination of prayer and practice. "Novena" comes from the Latin word for "nine." These prayer cycles are made up of nine straight days of prayer using either a rosary, a book of devotional prayers, or some other personalized practice. The history of the novena is somewhat complicated. Some scholars [source] believe it is adapted from Roman traditions of mourning for nine days after the death of a loved one. A more Biblical explanation focuses on the number nine and its significance in Scriptures. Nine is a holy number in many religious traditions, but in the Catholic tradition, nine is often seen as a number approaching perfection (represented by 10 in medieval Christian numerology). Nine is also the product of three and three, symbolizing the Trinity as infinite. Nine is also the number of months Mary carried Jesus in her womb, a period shared by all mothers and therefore holy around the globe. At the Crucifixion, Jesus dies on the ninth hour, another important occurrence of nine. According to tradition, one supported by the Conference of Bishops, the novena can be traced back to an episode in the Gospels where, after the Ascension, the Blessed Mother and the Apostles retreated to the Upper Room (the same place where the Last Supper occurred) to spend nine days fasting and praying until Pentecost, when the Holy Spirit descended upon them. Although not officially part of Church practice until Pius IX in (date), the novena has remained popular to this day, especially in Latin America.

Novenas are recited for three main reasons. First, they are often recited during periods of mourning, either before or after a funeral. This continues a tradition common in Greek and Roman cultures where a similar time frame was used to honor and pray for the dead. Second, novenas can be used as an intercessory to make a request of God and his [deputies]. This can include spiritual needs such as protection against evil influence or physical needs such as illness. For example, the novenas of St. Peregrine and St. Jude, two patron saints of those battling cancer, are intercessors with specific purposes. Third, they are most commonly used to prepare for Feast Days. Each Feast Day has an officially recognized novena.[71] Preparing for Feast Days is an excellent way to protect ourselves from evil interference because the combination of prayer, ritual, and fasting purifies both the body and spirit, making it far more difficult for demonic influence to penetrate our barriers. Even though satanic plots always threaten us, certain Feast Days provide an added level of protection. For example, All Saint's

---

[71] The official full calendar of novenas can be found here:
https://catholicnovenaapp.com/list-of-all-novenas/#

Day is an especially holy day when demonic entities struggle to affect us. High Feast Days, such as Christmas and Easter, are when demonic power is at its weakest, adding further protection in addition to any measures we may have taken to defend ourselves.

Sacred Objects

As mentioned in Part 3, sacred objects and icons provide even further protection. These include sacred symbols such as the crucifix, sacramentals such as holy water and chrism, blessed objects such as medallions and votive candles, and ritual instruments such as the Rosary. In addition, we will address the proper use of statuary, the components of an effective home altar, and rituals associated with sacred objects in practice.

The Crucifix and Christograms

No symbol is more repulsive to demons than the sight of the crucifix. As a reminder of the ultimate sacrifice of God for his Children, the image of the cross remains the central [image] of Christianity throughout the globe, much as the Star of David represents Judaism or the Crescent represents Islam. Regarding the sign of the cross, St. John Vianney once asserted, "The sign of the cross is the most terrible weapon against the devil. Thus the Church wishes not only that we have it continually in front of our minds to recall to us just what our souls are worth and what they cost Jesus Christ, but also that we should make it at every juncture ourselves: when we go to bed, when we awaken during the night, when we get up, when we begin any action, and, above all, when we are tempted." Catholic practice encourages both making the cross frequently as a gesture of protective blessing and placing physical crosses throughout one's home and workplace.

The Cross also represents our own sufferings and our means to salvation. "Apart from the cross," St. Rose of Lima once wrote, "there is no other ladder by which we may get to Heaven." Through our identification with Christ's suffering, we can transcend our own. At the same time, too often, we are the sources of our own suffering, although we frequently remain blind to this misfortune: "That we are generally the carpenters of our own crosses is a truth sadly easier to recognize in others than in ourselves" (St. Philip Neri).

A true crucifix depicts both the wooden cross itself as well as the crucified Jesus.

The most effective crucifixes have a hidden compartment inside that contains a phial of holy water, votive candles, and sometimes a piece of Eucharist. Above the figure of the crucified Christ, we often find a *titulus* with the letters INRI, a Latin abbreviation for *Iesus Nazarenus Rex Iudædorum* or "Jesus of Nazareth, King of the Jews." This references the plaque nailed above the Cross at the Crucifixion by the Romans (John 19:19; Mark 15:26; Matthew 27:37). Although meant to mock the condemned Christ, the title, in fact, reminds us of Jesus' status as the rightful heir to the throne of Israel through his descent from David, as well as his status as the King of Heaven and Son of God. Indeed, all the imagery from the Crucifixion intended to humiliate Christ—the Crown of Thorns, the purple garments of royalty, the Cross itself—have become sacred symbols of humankind's ultimate spiritual sacrifice and salvation.

Several other sacred symbols, known as Christograms, are worth mentioning here as they both operate in much the same way as the crucifix. The first is the chi-rho symbol . This sign combines the first two letters of "Christ," which is written in Greek as "Christos" or ΧΡΙΣΤΟΣ. This symbol is most famously associated with Emperor Constantine, who had a vision of the chi-rho before the Battle of Milvian Bridge in AD 213 and inscribed this Christogram on his army's shields. After the victory, Constantine converted to Christianity and soon after issued the monumental Edict of Milan, which established Christianity in the Roman Empire. This legend led to many legions adopting the chi-rho Christogram on banners, emblems, and shields, especially as conversion became widespread in the latter years of the imperial period. Today, the chi-rho remains a powerful ward against evil influence, one that can be inscribed upon objects to impart upon them some of the sacred power of Christ.

A similar Christogram is IHS or IHΣ, which comes from the first three letters of the name "Jesus" in Greek, which is spelled "Iesos." Like the chi-rho, this symbol invokes the name of Jesus in his capacity as the Son of God but also implies other meanings. In the Latin tradition, IHS was sometimes translated as an acronym for "In hoc signo," which is Latin for "in this sign." These were the words proclaimed by Constantine the Great before his victory at the Battle of Milvian Bridge, one of the most important events in the history of Christianity. As Constantine said, "In hoc signo vinces" ("In this sign I conquer"), so too can we use the IHS Christogram as a symbolic affirmation of our allegiance with Christ. Another interpretation identifies IHS with the Latin phrase "Iesus Hominum Salvator," meaning "Jesus, Savior of Humanity." Regardless of the interpretation, the symbol remains a powerful weapon against demonic influence.

A final symbol is the Alpha-Omega, one of the first to designate Christ in His role as the divine Son. Represented by the first and last letters of the Greek alphabet, the Alpha-Omega refers to Christ in His role as the beginning and the end of all things, a position he shares with God the Father. One of the earliest Christograms, the Alpha-Omega, appears in the Book of Revelation as a symbol of God (1:8; 21:6) and Christ (22:13). Christ also states in this same Scripture, "I am Alpha and

Omega, the first and the last" (1:11). Christ's words here in this apocalyptic text echo a similar claim from the Old Testament, where in Isaiah we read: "I am the first and I am the last; apart from me there is no God" (44:6). As a sign of Christ's unity with the Father, the Alpha-Omega also reinforces the eternal nature of Christ's power, and therefore the symbol grants us a connection to that very power.

The alpha alone remains a common sight on bumper stickers, where the alpha is often compared to a fish, referring to Jesus' words to the first apostles, Peter and Andrew, fishermen to whom he said, "I will make you fishers of men" (Mk 1:17, Mt 4:19). The connection with the image of a fish was further reinforced by Tertullian, one of the Fathers of the Church, who noted that the letters in the Greek word for fish *ichthys* also implied an anagram meaning "Jesus Christ, Son of God, Savior."[72] St. Augustine elaborates further in *The City of God*: "Of these five Greek words (Iesous, Christos, Theou, Uios, Soter), should you group together the letters, you would form the word ichthus, fish, the mystical name of Jesus the Christ who, in the abyss of our mortality, as though in the depths of the sea, was able to remain alive, that is, free from sin."[73] Especially when used in combination with the chi-rho— a practice common from the Middle Ages to today—the Alpha-Omega can serve us in spiritual warfare much like the chi-rho.

---

[72] *De Baptismo* 1 (2nd c.)
[73] *The City of God*, p. 23

All these Christograms—the crucifix, the chi-rho, the IHS, and the Alpha-Omega—provide us with wards against evil in much the same way that ancient runes were used to protect against negative energy. By inscribing objects with these symbols, we announce to both natural and supernatural observers that we are on the side of the Light, that we rebuke Satan, and that we are willing to fight any darkness that may attempt to intrude into our lives. Much like Constantine the Great, we can use these Christograms to strengthen our spiritual shields and reaffirm our awareness of God's love through Christ's ultimate sacrifice.

The Rosary

The rosary holds a special place in Catholic practice, though its origins and use remain unfamiliar to many outside the faith. As a combination of both prayer formula and ritual practice, the rosary provides a means for both meditation and protection. One important thing to note is that even though it takes the form of a necklace, the rosary should not be worn around the neck, mainly because it disrespects the sacred tool as a simple ornamental piece of jewelry instead of a spiritual conduit between us and the divine. The act of saying the rosary follows a distinct set of rules based on the beads of the rosary itself and their arrangement.[74] The rosary is powerful both as a sacred

---

[74] The US Conference of Catholic Bishops provides a great guide on reciting the rosary on its official website: https://www.usccb.org/how-to-pray-the-rosary

object and a prayer formula. During exorcisms, priests carry a rosary with them in addition to a crucifix. Reciting the rosary is a tool used by many exorcists to cast out demonic entities. Importantly, praying the crucifix can be done either alone or as part of a group. Reciting the rosary in a group magnifies its positive effects.

The Rosary has played an important role in spiritual warfare throughout the Tradition. St. Teresa of Avila strongly advocated reciting the rosary to fight off demonic attacks, as did St. John of the Cross. An especially convincing example of the Rosary's power comes from Blessed Bartolo Longo, the reformed satanic priest later canonized in the 20th century. After his struggles with Satanism, Longo converted when he experienced a vision of the Blessed Mother, who instructed him to seek salvation in the Rosary. When he was ordained, Bartolo took the name of Rosario to honor the amazing spiritual power of the Rosary. He later composed a prayer specifically addressed to Mary in her role as Our Lady of the Rosary:

O blessed rosary of Mary, sweet chain which unites us to God,

Bond of love which unites us to the angels,

Tower of salvation against the assaults of Hell,

Safe port in our universal shipwreck,

We will never abandon you.

You will be our comfort in the hour of death;

Yours our final kiss as life ebbs away.

And the last words from our lips will be your sweet name,

O Queen of the Rosary of Pompeii,

O dearest, Mother, O Refuge of Sinners,

O Sovereign Consoler of the Afflicted.

May you be everywhere blessed, today and always,

On earth and in Heaven.

- Amen.

There are a few rules to follow when reciting the rosary. First, the rosary should be held in the left hand with the right hand used for running along the beads. This reflects our acknowledgment that Christ sits at God's right hand. Second, praying the rosary is most effective when done out loud. In fact, according to Gregorian practice, singing the rosary magnifies the power of the ritual. This reflects a meditation traditionally attributed to St. Augustine of Hippo that *"bis orat qui cantat"* or "he who sings prays twice."[75] A similar call to singing appears in

---

[75] This statement is somewhat apocryphal, though Augustine does address the power of song in *Confessions* IX:6-14 and X: 33-49).

Paul's letters to the Ephesians (5:19) and Colossians (3:16) encouraging the use of hymns and psalms. Monks in the Gregorian Order have integrated these principles into their rosary practice, which is sung in unison using the well-known Gregorian chant. The result is a combination of beauty and sacred intention that amplifies the blessings received when we recite the rosary.

The rosary is divided into sections. The crucifix, the first "major" bead (representing God), the three "minor" beads (representing the Trinity), the Glory Bead (representing the Trinity as "three in one"), and five "decades" of ten "minor" beads with a "major" bead separating each decade.

According to the Conference of Bishops, reciting the rosary should follow this formula:

Make the Sign of the Cross.

Holding the Crucifix, say the *Apostles' Creed.*

On the first bead, say an *Our Father.*

Say one *Hail Mary* on each of the next three beads.

Say the *Glory Be*

For each of the five decades, announce the Mystery (perhaps followed by a brief reading from Scripture) then say the *Our Father.*

While fingering each of the ten beads of the decade, next say ten Hail Marys while meditating on the Mystery. Then say a *Glory Be.*

(After finishing each decade, some say the following prayer requested by the Blessed Virgin Mary at Fatima: O my Jesus, forgive us our sins, save us from the fires of hell; lead all souls to Heaven, especially those who have most need of your mercy.)

After saying the five decades, say the Hail, Holy Queen, followed by this dialogue and prayer:

V. Pray for us, O holy Mother of God.

R. That we may be made worthy of the promises of Christ.

Let us pray: O God, whose Only Begotten Son, by his life, Death, and Resurrection, has purchased for us the rewards of eternal life, grant, we beseech thee, that while meditating on these mysteries of the most holy Rosary of the Blessed Virgin Mary, we may imitate what they contain and obtain what they promise, through the same Christ our Lord. Amen.

(A prayer to St. Joseph may also follow.)

Conclude the Rosary with the Sign of the Cross.

The Four Mysteries

The Four Mysteries of the Rosaries are an extension of this formula, where after each decade of beads, a Mystery is proclaimed followed by an *Our Father*.

The Four Mysteries of the Rosary are The Joyful, The Sorrowful, The Glorious, and the Luminous. The last is a recent addition, made official by St. John Paul II in 2002 during his time as pope. These Mysteries are connected to the Liturgical Calendar, with each Mystery belonging to specific days of the weeks and ecclesiastical seasons such as Lent and Advent.

Each of the Mysteries is further divided, each with its own "fruit," or blessing. This is a reference to both the "fruit" of Mary's womb (i.e., Jesus) as well as the Fruit of Knowledge in Eden, the sin of which was washed away by Christ's sacrifice. These fruits are also symbolic of the fruit of the vine, a reference to the Blood of Christ as wine.

The Joyful Mysteries

Traditionally recited on Mondays, Saturdays, and Sundays during Advent, the Five Joyful Mysteries are based on wondrous events in the Gospels. The first is The Annunciation when the Archangel Gabriel visited Mary and told her that she had been chosen to bear the Son of God (Luke 1:26-28). The fruit of this

Mystery is humility. The second Joyful Mystery is the Visitation when the Holy Spirit stirred Christ in the womb, and Elizabeth proclaimed that Mary was "Most blessed are you among women, and blessed is the fruit of your womb" (Luke 1:39-42). The third Joyful Mystery is the Nativity (Luke 2:1-7), the event of Christ's birth celebrated at Christmas. The fruit of this Mystery is poverty, bringing us to a closer awareness of the poor in the world and our role to help them in their struggle. The fourth Joyful Mystery is the Presentation in the Temple, when the adolescent Jesus explained the ways of God to a group of rabbis and scholars in Jerusalem, amazing them with his understanding of the Divine (Luke 2:21-29). The fruit of this Mystery is purity of heart and body. The fifth and final Joyful Mystery is the Finding in the Temple when Joseph finds his stepson instructing the elders (Luke 2:41-47). The fruit of this Mystery is devotion to Jesus.

The Sorrowful Mysteries

Traditionally recited on Tuesdays, Fridays, and Sundays during Lent, the Sorrowful Mysteries of the Rosary recount the struggles of Christ in the Gospels. Through contemplation of these trials, we come to a greater understanding of the power of sacrifice and the need for suffering as a path toward redemption. We all suffer, and when demonic influences penetrate our lives, this suffering can lead to despair. Instead of submitting to this despair, we can use that suffering to grow closer to Christ and accept His light into our lives. As a result, the demonic attempts to torture us are washed away.

The Agony in the Garden

"Then Jesus came with them to a place called Gethsemane, and he said to his disciples, 'Sit here while I go over there and pray.' He took along Peter and the two sons of Zebedee, and began to feel sorrow and distress. Then he said to them, 'My soul is sorrowful even to death. Remain here and keep watch with me.' He advanced a little and fell prostrate in prayer, saying, 'My Father, if it is possible, let this cup pass from me; yet, not as I will, but as you will.'"

- Matthew 26:36-39

The first Sorrowful Mystery, the Agony in the Garden, recalls Jesus' struggle in the Garden of Gethsemane on the night Pilate's soldiers arrested him. As he contemplates the sacrifice ahead of him, he struggles with doubts, showing that Jesus is both God and the Son of Man. In order to truly experience the depths of human suffering, Jesus questions his own sacred mission but finds within Himself the strength to submit himself to the trials awaiting him. The fruit of this Mystery is obedience to God's Will. Just as Jesus submitted Himself to the Divine Plan, so too must we if we are to empower ourselves with His grace. Obedience implies not only submission but also loyalty.

When we demonstrate our loyalty to the Light, we pledge ourselves to the righteous cause.

The Scourging at the Pillar

"Then he released Barabbas to them, but after he had Jesus scourged, he handed him over to be crucified."

- Matthew 27:26

The Second Sorrowful Mystery recalls the suffering of Christ when he is tied to a pillar and brutally scourged by Roman soldiers before his trial. The physical injuries endured by Christ during this event weakened Him tremendously but only strengthened His resolve. Symbolically, Christ's scourging represents the daily troubles we all face. We are reminded to follow Christ's lead and use these trials as sources of spiritual courage and not let the pain of life weaken us to Satan's will.

The fruit of this Mystery is Mortification. Although not as widely practiced today, mortification was a central practice in many medieval Christian sects. The most notable form of this physical demonstration of piety is flagellation, a direct homage to the Scourging at the Pillar. In certain contemporary Christian traditions, especially in the Philippines and Central America, flagellation continues very much unchanged from the medieval practice. Using leather whips, or flagella, the faithful undertake pilgrimages, often on their knees, while lashing themselves across the back and reciting devotional prayers. Brutal as it may seem, the practice stems from a litany of similar practices, such as the wearing of hair shirts among certain monastic orders, the use of Procrustean Beds, and by extension the practice of fasting. By depriving the body of physical strength, we can often transmit vigor into the spirit.

The Crowning with Thorns

"Then the soldiers of the governor took Jesus inside the praetorium and gathered the whole cohort around him. They stripped off his clothes and threw a scarlet military cloak about him. Weaving a crown out of thorns, they placed it on his head, and a reed in his right hand. And kneeling before him, they mocked him, saying, 'Hail, King of the Jews!'"

- Matthew 27:27-29

The Crown of Thorns remains one of the most enduring symbols of Christianity. Humiliated by Roman soldiers, Christ is crowned with a gruesome [diadem], an attempt to mock Him in His role as the King of the Jews. However, the Crown marks yet another moment of suffering in Christ's path to the Cross. In the same way, the Crown of Thorns represents all the suffering life throws our way. As the poet, Percy Shelley once noted, "I fall on the thorns of life! I bleed!"[76] Likewise, St. Paul the Apostle noted his struggle with "a thorn in the flesh" (2 Cor.

---

[76] Shelley, P.B. "Ode to the West Wind" (1820), line 54.

12:7). We all face our personal Crown of Thorns at some point in our lives, a moment of pain and ridicule. In those moments, we must embrace the fruit of this Mystery: Courage. Remember that courage is one of the cardinal virtues, a golden mean between foolhardiness and cowardice. When we summon the courage to confront the obstacles in our life, we are walking in the footsteps of Christ. When we acknowledge our shortcomings and refuse to give up, we embrace his courage. When we think all hope is lost, we can draw upon the infinite love of Christ within us and carry on through any Hell.

The Carrying of the Cross

"They pressed into service a passer-by, Simon, a Cyrenian, who was coming in from the country, the father of Alexander and Rufus, to carry his cross. They brought him to the place of Golgotha (which is translated Place of the Skull)."

- Mark 15:21-22

The Cross symbolizes all humanity's sins. As the final test of Christ's faith in God the Father, the Cross stands for all our burdens, especially those of the spirit. The tale of St. Simon of Cyrene—another powerful intercessor in matters of spiritual warfare—is one that should inspire us toward charity and self-sacrifice. Even though he did not know Jesus, Simon of Cyrene took up the Cross for Him when he could no longer carry it.

This act of charity brought Simon under the Roman lash himself but also showed that strangers can come to our aid if they too embrace the goodwill of Christian virtue. Moreover, Simon was patient, refusing to curse the soldiers or his misfortune at being pulled from the crowd to carry this terrible weight. For this reason, the Fruit of this Sorrowful Mystery is patience, a virtue more vital than perhaps ever before. To truly maintain our victory over the Darkness, we must practice patience. This is especially true in today's modern world of technological distractions and hectic daily routines. When we practice patience, we reset our focus where it truly matters.

The Crucifixion and Death

"When they came to the place called the Skull, they crucified him and the criminals there, one on his right, the other on his left. [Then Jesus said, 'Father, forgive them, they know not what they do.'] They divided his garments by casting lots. The people stood by and watched; the rulers, meanwhile, sneered at him and said, 'He saved others, let him save himself if he is the chosen one, the Messiah of God.' Even the soldiers jeered at him. As they approached to offer him wine they called out, 'If you are King of the Jews, save yourself.' Above him there was an inscription that read, 'This is the King of the Jews.' Now one of the criminals hanging there reviled Jesus, saying, 'Are you not the Messiah? Save yourself and us.' The other, however, rebuking him, said in reply, 'Have you no fear of God, for you are subject to the same condemnation? And indeed, we have been condemned justly, for the sentence we received corresponds to our crimes, but this man

has done nothing criminal.' Then he said, 'Jesus, remember me when you come into your kingdom.' He replied to him, 'Amen, I say to you, today you will be with me in Paradise.'

"It was now about noon and darkness came over the whole land until three in the afternoon because of an eclipse of the sun. Then the veil of the temple was torn down the middle. Jesus cried out in a loud voice, 'Father, into your hands I commend my spirit'; and when he had said this he breathed his last."

- Luke 23:33-46

No other image sums up the Christian faith than the Crucifixion. Without this ultimate sacrifice whereby God demonstrated His love for humanity by giving the life of His son, there could be no Resurrection. Likewise, without our own suffering, without our own admission of our mortality, we cannot enter into a state of Grace. To know true forgiveness, we must know suffering. The Fruit of this Mystery, sorrow for our sins, implores us to grieve for Christ's death even as we reassure ourselves that He will return. Christ, in his capacity as the Lamb of God, offered up His own life so that our spirits might live on through him eternally. This is God's ultimate gift to humanity, the fulfillment of His promises to Noah, Abraham, and Moses that he would never abandon us, even in death. The Death of Christ is, therefore, in some ways the Death of Sin, and when we accept that truth, we strengthen ourselves against demons, agents of sin itself.

Glorious Mysteries

Traditionally recited on Wednesdays and Sundays in Ordinary Time, the Five Glorious Mysteries recount the more spectacular events in Christ's life, death, and resurrection. When we recite the Glorious Mysteries during the Rosary, we surround ourselves with the miraculous aspects of Christ, the great enemy of the Prince of Darkness.

The Resurrection

"But at daybreak on the first day of the week they took the spices they had prepared and went to the tomb. They found the stone rolled away from the tomb; but when they entered, they did not find the body of the Lord Jesus. While they were puzzling over this, behold, two men in dazzling garments appeared to them. They were terrified and bowed their faces to the ground. They said to them, 'Why do you seek the living one among the dead? He is not here, but he has been raised.'"

- Luke 24:1-5

The Resurrection is the essence of the New Covenant. By showing us that death is not the end, Christ empowers us in our lives. He frees us from any fear of death or doubt in God's love for us once our mortal mission has ended. Of all the miracles in the Gospels, the Resurrection ranks first, the ultimate demonstration of God's power. This Glorious Mystery also calls upon us to toss aside doubt. In the Acts of the Apostles, we read that even St. Thomas, an apostle close to Jesus throughout His ministry, doubted that Christ really had returned from the dead. Only when he put his hand into the wounds of the Messiah was he convinced, instantly repenting of his doubt. We must resist the temptation to doubt as Thomas did and fortify ourselves with the Fruit of the Mystery, Faith. Faith in the Resurrected Jesus is a direct rejection of Satan, who toiled to prevent God from demonstrating His power through such a miracle. In its role as one of the Four Horsemen of the Apocalypse, Death—that is physical *and* spiritual death for unbelievers—often operates on Satan's behalf as a force of destruction. But when we recall the Resurrection, we deny the power of Death over us and accept the gift of eternal life at God's side.

The Ascension

"So, then the Lord Jesus, after he spoke to them, was taken up into heaven and took his seat at the right hand of God."

- Mark 16:19

The Ascension remains one of the most profound events in the Gospels. After his death and resurrection, Christ affirms to His disciples that the prophecies have been fulfilled. However, His mission accomplished, He cannot remain on Earth but must instead return to His rightful place at the Right Hand of His Father. As He bids farewell to his disciples, Christ is assumed into Heaven by the Divine Host, ascending to his celestial throne body and soul. This Glorious Mystery brings with it the Fruit of Hope. Just as Christ ascended into Heaven, so too, at the moment of our own deaths, we can hope for the blessing of God and, if our spirits are pure and our hearts unburdened, ascend ourselves into the Kingdom of God. Meditating on this hope through the Rosary, therefore, dispels Satan's temptation for us to doubt and despair. The Enemy wants us to fear death, doubt our immortal souls' sacred destiny, and abandon our belief in the Life Everlasting. Rejecting these tools of evil, in turn, repels those demonic forces attempting to sow them in our minds.

The Descent of the Holy Spirit

"When the time for Pentecost was fulfilled, they were all in one place together. And suddenly there came from the sky a noise like a strong driving wind, and it filled the entire house in which they were. Then there appeared to them tongues as of fire, which parted and came to rest on each one of them. And they were all filled with the holy Spirit and began to speak in different tongues, as the Spirit enabled them to proclaim."

- Acts 2:1-4

Pentecost once held a much more important place in the

Catholic calendar than it currently does, yet observing this high holy feast day is a means of reaffirming our alliance with the Holy Spirit. Pentecost commemorates the descent of the Holy Spirit upon the Apostles after the Ascension of Christ, giving them the ability to spread the Gospel in many languages. This Glorious Mystery is also related to one of the charismatic gifts of the Holy Spirit, the gift of tongues. This gift plays a role in encounters with demonic entities, for a person blessed with the gift of tongues can often interpret what others cannot. This is especially true during exorcisms when demonic entities often speak in languages unknown to those around them. However, if a charismatic with the gift of tongues is present, they may be able to use this gift of the Holy Spirit to translate the demon's words and give the exorcist (if he is not, in fact, the one with the gift himself, which is sometimes the case) more insight into the demon's motivations and intentions. The Fruit of the Mystery, Wisdom, is, therefore, an extension of this gift, a power to distinguish the Will of God from the deceits of the Prince of Lies.

The Assumption

"Behold, from now on will all ages call me blessed. The Mighty One has done great things for me, and holy is his name."

- Luke 1:48-49

The Assumption holds a special place in the Catholic tradition, one that is not shared by many other Christian denominations. According to the Catechism, the Virgin Mary was assumed, body and soul, into Heaven and did not suffer a human death. This Glorious Mystery represents the fulfillment of the prophecies foretold by God in the Old Testament, the promise of salvation and a New Covenant. Above all else, Mary was humble before God, never once taking for granted the special blessing given to her. Devotion to Mary, the Fruit of the Mystery, rests at the center of the Rosary itself since as we proceed through the decades of beads, we remind ourselves of her place in our lives as Mother and Protector.

The Coronation of Mary

"A great sign appeared in the sky, a woman clothed with the sun, with the moon under her feet, and on her head a crown of twelve stars."

- Revelation 12:1

The Coronation of Mary is another special Mystery because it reinforces the Virgin Mary's role as the Queen of Heaven and nemesis of Satan. Her crown establishes her place in the Heavenly Court, a place formerly occupied by Lucifer before his betrayal. Her throne beside her Son forces Satan to remember what he lost through his pride, a loss that brought with it eternal separation from God's love. The Fruit of this Mystery is the grace of a happy death, for Mary, in her protection, assures us that our spirits will make their way to the Divine if we practice virtue, righteousness, and live as Christ did for our fellow human beings. Satan, in his plots against us, wants us to doubt this gift of salvation and instead submit to fear. In turn, fear leads us toward sin and the possibility of damnation if we abandon hope.

Luminous Mysteries

The most recent addition to the canonical rosary, the Five Luminous Mysteries, are to be recited on Thursdays. Pope John Paul II officially established these Mysteries as part of the Mystery of the Rosary, recalling miraculous moments in Christ's life that remain relevant in our spiritual lives.

The Baptism of Christ in the Jordan

"After Jesus was baptized, he came up from the water and behold, the heavens were opened [for him], and he saw the Spirit of God descending like a dove [and] coming upon him. And a voice came from the heavens, saying, 'This is my beloved Son, with whom I am well pleased.'"

- Matthew 3:16-17

The Baptism of Christ in Jordan marks the beginning of His ministry and the arrival of the Holy Spirit. The form of the dove taken by the Holy Spirit is important as it calls to mind the dove which brought the olive branch to Noah as the Flood subsided to let him know that God had not abandoned him. The spiritual purification involved in Baptism washes away Original Sin, yet for Jesus—who was born of the Virgin Mary (herself Immaculately conceived without Original Sin) and the Father, eternally good—this ritual signified his role as the Messiah come to save humanity from sin. When we recite these verses from Matthew during the Rosary and contemplate the Luminous Mystery involved, we reflect on both our own acceptance of Christ through Baptism and the protections this acceptance provides against the workings of Satan. Fittingly, the Fruit of this Mystery is openness to the Holy Spirit, for, through Baptism, we recognize the Father as our Creator, the Son as our Savior, and the Holy Spirit as the sacred fire of the Divine present in all who uphold the Path of Light.

The Wedding Feast at Cana

"On the third day there was a wedding in Cana in Galilee, and the mother of Jesus was there. Jesus and his disciples were also invited to the wedding. When the wine ran short, the mother of Jesus said to him, 'They have no wine.' [And] Jesus said to her, 'Woman, how does your concern affect me? My hour has not yet come.' His mother said to the servers, 'Do whatever he tells you.'"

- John 2:1-5

In the Gospel of John, the Wedding at Cana tells the story of one of Christ's more memorable miracles. During the celebration feast, the celebrants run out of wine. To demonstrate his generosity and divinity, Christ then transforms pitchers of water into wine at the feast. This practice of transmutation, replicated in the transubstantiation of bread and wine into body and blood during the Eucharist, reminds us that through Christ's power, we can transform ourselves from fallible human beings into more perfect vessels for the sacred. The Fruit of this Mystery is the access to Jesus through Mary, a profound realization in matters of spiritual warfare given Mary's supreme status as an enemy of all things demonic. Just as Jesus transformed water into wine, our prayers to Mary are transformed and transmitted to her Son.

Jesus' Proclamation of the Coming of the Kingdom of God

"'This is the time of fulfillment. The kingdom of God is at hand. Repent, and believe in the gospel.'"

- Mark 1:15

When Jesus proclaims the Coming of the Kingdom in the Gospel of Mark, we are called to be witnesses. By acknowledging the supremacy of the Creator and the saving power of Grace through Christ, we open ourselves to this Luminous Mystery where Christ promises us salvation if we repent of our sins. As Daniel B. Lancaster notes in his spiritual warfare prayer manual, "Repentance is a powerful prayer weapon in the war room, because our hearts are hard and need to be soft towards God"[77]. The Fruit of this Mystery, conversion, comes not simply in the form of a one-time event, but instead as a lifelong process of affirmation. Through this affirmation, we empower ourselves against the wiles of Satan because we understand fully that Christ's Kingdom can never be overthrown by the Prince of Darkness.

The Transfiguration

The Transfiguration is an often-misunderstood event in the Gospels. Taking the Apostles Peter, John, and James with him atop a mountain, Christ revealed to them a glimpse of His divine nature: "And he was transfigured before them; his face shone like the sun and his clothes became white as light" (Mt. 17:1-2). This Luminous Mystery calls upon us to recognize Christ's divinity even as we see the divine in ourselves and those around us. We are all reflections of Christ, capable of transfiguring ourselves as we grow closer to the Source of All Things. Appropriately, the Fruit of the Mystery, the Desire for Holiness, is an invitation that draws us closer to an understanding of how we can open ourselves to the glorious benevolence of Christ. This relates directly to the importance of setting intentions in

---

[77] Lancaster, D. *Powerful Prayers in the War Room: Learning to Pray Like a Powerful Prayer Warrior* (2015)

spiritual warfare situations. To effectively combat the demonic, we must express a sincere desire to sanctify ourselves.

The Institution of the Eucharist

"While they were eating, Jesus took bread, said the blessing, broke it, and giving it to his disciples said, 'Take and eat; this is my body.'"

- Matthew 26:26

The final Luminous Mystery recalls the Institution of the Eucharist at the Last Supper. When Jesus gathered his disciples together at the Cenacle or Upper Room, he pledged to them that He would always be with them. At the Last Supper, Christ also revealed the central mystery of the Faith, which is the transubstantiation of bread and wine into body and blood so that through the Sacrament of the Eucharist we can partake in the sacred essence of Christ Himself. We ingest not mere bread and wine but participate in a ritual established by Christ to commemorate his sacrifice and unite ourselves as the metaphorical body of Christ, the Church, and all the faithful. The Fruit of this Mystery calls for adoration, and we recite this Mystery during the Rosary to demonstrate our adoration for the miraculous deeds performed by God through Christ, both during his life and throughout our own. Adoring Christ and his works in this way infuriates Satan, of course, who refused to bow in adoration before Adam and who constantly wants our praise for himself.

Holy Water

As we saw in the Rite of Major Exorcism, holy water is an essential component for expelling the most serious cases of demonic interference. The tradition itself dates back to the earliest days of the Church. According to the 5th century *Apostolic Constitutions,* the practice of blessing water for ritual use in the Church originated with St. Matthew. As a symbol of purification, water is used in accordance with previous uses in the Judaic tradition. The power of holy water in spiritual warfare cannot be overstated. St. Teresa of Avila described it as the mightiest weapon against the demonic. More recently, Tanquedec described it as repelling from both places and people "all the power of the enemy and the enemy himself and his apostate angels."[78] Whether as a protective or an aggressive option, holy water is a staple in our arsenal.

First and foremost, holy water recalls the Baptism of Christ in the River Jordan. As we discussed in our exploration of the Mysteries of the Rosary, this was the moment when the Holy Spirit descended upon Jesus, confirming him to his cousin John the Baptist and his disciples that Jesus was, in fact, the Messiah. In the same way, when water is blessed by a priest in his capacity

---

[78] Tonquedec p. 50

as *in persona Christi*, the liquid is infused with sacred power. The first recorded instance of blessing water in this way comes from the writings of the 4th-century bishop Serapion of Thumis, who included a prayer formula for the blessing in his Pontifical.[79] Since most early baptisms in the Church were performed using waters in rivers, lakes, and seas, a need for blessing water in baptisteries inspired Serapion's formula. The blessing applies to both water and oil (chrism), reading: "We bless these creatures in the Name of Jesus Christ, Thy only Son; we invoke upon this water and this oil the Name of Him Who suffered, Who was crucified, Who arose from the dead, and Who sits at the right of the Uncreated. Grant unto these creatures the power to heal; may all fevers, every evil spirit, and all maladies be put to flight by him who either drinks these beverages or is anointed with them, and may they be a remedy in the name of Jesus Christ, Thy only Son." This blessing ritual is intended to be performed during the Mass.

Instances of the use of holy water as a protective substance and weapon against demonic entities are common in early Church history. In *Contra Haeres* by St. Epiphanius, we read about an early Christian named Joseph who cast a demon from an afflicted man by making the sign of the cross and poured water over him, reciting the formula "In the name of Jesus Christ of Nazareth, crucified, depart from this unhappy one, thou infernal spirit, and let him be healed!" Interestingly, the Joseph mentioned in this account was not an early bishop or priest but

---

[79] This formula also appears in the 4th/5th century Syriac text *Testamentum Domini*.

merely a devout Christian. Blessing water in this fashion was later used in the Middle Ages to confront demonic influences. St. Gregory of Tours recounts many examples of this practice as well.[80] In many cases, the holy water in St. Gregory's accounts is drunk by the afflicted, a practice that is much less common today.

There is, of course, an elemental consideration to be made here as well. Demons, by their very nature, are creatures associated with hellfire, in many ways the polar opposite of holy water. This potent repellent property goes beyond baptismal water alone, extending to the holy water used in other ways. This partially explains why Pope Leo IV mandated that every Sunday, the officiating priest should bless water and splash (a process technically called "aspersion") it on the congregation during Mass. Holy water is also placed in the vestibule of Catholic churches for use by the faithful in blessing themselves. This act serves as a purification before entering the nave. The practice of blessing the water before Mass was first described by Hincmar of Reims in *Capitula Synodalia*, a medieval supplementary text for the faithful. Although the time and location of blessing water varies from parish to parish, the practice is generally performed by clergy in the sacristy of the Church before Mass on Sundays. Two exceptions to this rule are Easter and Pentecost, partly because the day before these holy feasts, the water used in baptismal fonts is consecrated for

---

[80] De gloria confess., c. 82; ("De Miraculis S. Martini", II, xxxix; "Mirac. S. Juliani", II, iii, xxv, xxvi; "Liber de Passione S. Juliani"; "Vitae Patrum", c. iv, n. 3

the year's sacraments.

In modern practice, holy water serves three primary functions. The first is repentance since the sacramental recalls the sacrament of Baptism. The purification function of holy water finds its source in the Old Testament, where we read in Psalm 50, "O God, in your goodness, in the greatness of your compassion wipe out my offense. Thoroughly wash me from my guilt and of my sin cleanse me." When John the Baptist called upon the people of Judea to repent, he resorted to this same ritual, repeated when priests sprinkled holy water on the congregation during certain Masses.

The second function is protective. Holy water serves as a reminder to any potential threat that they are facing someone reinforced with the power of the divine. One of the earliest champions of using holy water for protection against evil energies was St. Teresa of Avila, a noted intercessor in spiritual warfare situations. As she noted in 1562, "From long experience I have learned that there is nothing like holy water to put devils to flight and prevent them from coming back again. They also flee from the Cross, but return; so holy water must have great virtue."[81] Thus, even though crucifixes and medallions may repel an evil spirit, holy water both repels and protects, making it unique among the sacramentals.

The third and final function of holy water in modern practice is

---

[81] St. Teresa of Avila notatum.

in its use in the actual Sacrament of Baptism. This ritual of purification and renewal makes a forceful point of rejecting Satan and his works, denying his lies, and refusing to doubt the ultimate power of the Almighty. In many senses, when we partake of holy water as a sacramental, we are reliving and reaffirming our own baptism in the Holy Spirit.

Chrism

A much less common—though extremely potent—protective substance is chrism. The connection between "chrism" and "Christ" is an important one, as "Christ" is the Greek translation of the Hebrew "meshiach" or "messiah," which literally means "anointed one." This ritual of anointing refers to the anointing of kings, relevant to Christ in his roles as both the King of the Jews (through his descent from David) and King of Heaven (through his station as the Son of God within the Trinity). Christ the King stands in direct opposition to Satan, the Prince of Hell, who, despite his prideful intentions and manipulations, can never achieve the status of king, doomed to a struggle that will ultimately fail.[82]

In modern practice, chrism is holy oil blessed by a clergy member, imbued with sanctifying grace. Its origins go back beyond the New Testament, and cultures worldwide have long

---

[82] See Revelation in NT.

placed significance on oil. In the Greek tradition, oil was often used during rituals and sacrifices. In the Roman tradition, oil and wine both played important parts in ritual practice, especially rites to the gods Apollo and Dionysus—deities that contributed many of their aspects to Christ in the early Church.

Chrism appears repeatedly in Scripture as well. In Exodus, we are told that Moses received instruction from God about consecrating priests: "Take the anointing oil and pour it on his [Aaron, brother of Moses] and anoint him" (29:7). In the Book of Samuel, we likewise hear God announce the anointment of the young David, destined to be King of Israel: "The Lord said: 'There—anoint him, for this is the one!' Then Samuel, with the horn of oil in hand, anointed him in the midst of his brothers, and from that day on, the spirit of the Lord rushed upon David" (1 Samuel 16:12-13). Since David was the youngest of his father Jesse's sons, his anointing also demonstrates the practice as one of sacred selection. David recalls this point in his psalms, singing, "Therefore your God has anointed you with the oil of gladness above your fellow kings" (Ps. 45:8). This anointing would later confirm David's descendant Jesus as the King of Kings.

As both anointed and anointer, Christ is thus chosen by God and assigned to spread His sacred gifts by anointing others. When Christ sends the Apostles out into the Levant to spread the Good News, heal the sick, and exorcise the possessed, he explicitly mentions anointing with oil: "And He called the twelve to Him, and began to send them out two by two, and gave them power over unclean spirits…And they cast out many demons, and anointed with oil many who were sick, and healed them" (Mark 6:7-13). The healing power of chrism finds its roots in Scripture, but anointing is also a call to service. As Jesus notes in the Gospel of Luke, "The Spirit of the Lord is upon me, because he has anointed me to bring glad tidings to the poor" (Luke 4:18). When we accept anointment, we accept our role as warriors in Christ's armies pitted against all forms of injustice, sin, and the workings of Satan.

This practice of anointment continues in the Sacraments. During Baptism, the [candidate] is anointed with chrism in the form of a cross on their forehead. This ritual act provides a lifelong barrier for the anointed, placing them under the protection of Christ and the armies of Heaven. Similarly, during the Sacrament of Confirmation, the officiant (usually, though not necessarily, the bishop of the candidate's diocese) anoints the candidate with holy oil and asks them to renew their baptismal vows. Then, the officiant affirms the transfer of grace, stating, "Be sealed with the gift of the Holy Spirit, recalling Paul's words: 'The one who gives us security with you in Christ and who anointed us is God. He has also put his seal upon us and given the Spirit in our hearts as a first installment' (2 Cor. 1:21-22). As the Catechism affirms, "This seal of the Holy Spirit marks our total belonging to Christ, our enrollment in his service forever, as well as the promise of divine protection in the great eschatological trial" (*CCC* No. 1296). This sacrament generates a particularly potent shield against evil influence as it reinforces the barrier provided by baptism. In addition, during the Sacrament of Confirmation, the candidate assumes their "confirmation name," a saint's name intended to create a bond between them and their chosen saint. This bond provides a source of sacred power between a specific benevolent spirit and the confirmed. Much like a guardian angel, the saint of confirmation offers protection, guidance, and intercessory influence in times of spiritual need.

Chrism is also used in two other major Catholic rituals: the Sacrament of Extreme Unction (also known as Last Rites) and the Rite of Major Exorcism. In the Sacrament of Extreme Unction, the dying individual is blessed with chrism in the sign of the cross on the forehead, followed by readings from Scripture and invocations to God to assist the departing soul on its journey. As we discussed earlier, a similar act is undertaken during exorcisms, when the priest blesses the afflicted person's forehead similarly. Both rituals are intended to provide spiritual protection in times of crisis, and both generate strong spiritual barricades against potential corruption by demonic interferences.

Candles

Candles have been a staple of religious ritual since prehistoric man first sensed the Divine in fire. Catholic practice draws on this ancient tradition, specifically through Judaic practice. In the Temple at Jerusalem, a candle continuously burned to symbolize that God was present (Lev. 24: 2-4). Likewise symbolizing God's presence, the Tabernacle on the Catholic altar is flanked by two lit candles before the Eucharist. The candle's flame also recalls Christ's role as dispeller of darkness. As we read in John's Gospel, Christ said, "I am the light of the world. No follower of mine shall ever walk in darkness; no, he shall possess the light of life" (8:12). He later emphasizes this point by proclaiming, "I have come to the world as its light, to keep anyone who believes in me from remaining in the dark" (John 12:46). When we are baptized, and when we participate in the Sacraments through our life of faith, we are reminded that Christ is the Light of the World, enemy of Satan, and redeemer of all spiritual darkness.

St. Francis of Assisi once claimed, "All the darkness in the world cannot extinguish the light of a single candle." This statement is a testament to the symbolic power of candles in the Tradition. Two primary types of candles exist in the Catholic Church: vigil and votive. Vigil candles are generally lit over a stretch of hours or days as a symbol of the faithful's devotion to the Lord. As we discussed earlier, "vigil" gives us the word "vigilance" via the Latin word *vigilia,* meaning "to keep watch." Vigil candles are most commonly used to commemorate the departed, but they can also be used in conjunction with saintly statues.

Votive candles are a mainstay of Catholic places of worship as well as home altars. Votive candles come in two varieties: those dedicated to saintly benefactors and those dedicated to the Deceased. The former are long cylindrical glass tubes with an image of the saint, angel, or Christ imprinted on the outside. Popular images include the Blessed Mother, St. Joseph, St. Francis, and the popes. The latter are most often found in churches and serve as a memorial for those who have passed beyond the veil.

The spiritual benefits of votive candles are amplified when used in conjunction with sacred statuary. This practice dates to the earliest days of Christianity, as St. Jerome notes in his late 4th-early 5th-century treatise *Contra Vigilantium* where the faithful often placed votive candles in front of images of saints and martyrs, as well as to commemorate the dead. A related practice was outlined in the 6th century by St. Radigund, who describes a ritual called "measuring to a saint," where the devoted light candles equal to their height in an act of solidarity with the specified saint.

Where and how to place votive candles varies by tradition. Many Hispanic faithful keep elaborate home altars with votive candles dedicated to various saints, most commonly the Blessed Mother in one of her many forms. Votive candles are generally lit to coincide with an act of prayer, intercessory or otherwise. This practice is taken to an extreme in some of the hybrid spiritual traditions, such as Santeria and Voodoo, which use votive candles extensively in their rituals.

Statuary

Statues feature prominently in Catholic worship, present at religious sites and shrines the world over. Many of these statues serve as templates for copies for use in and around the home. Although not necessarily blessed officially, statues of saints and other benevolent intercessors have a long tradition. Some of the greatest statues in the history of art take as their subjects the events of Scripture, the lives of the saints, and the glory of the angels.

Although many Protestant traditions did away with statues as a form of idolatry, the practice continues among Catholics as a means of acknowledging a saint or angel's power as well as using them as wards against evil. The use of statues, therefore, is *not* equivalent to worshipping the statue as a god. Instead, using statues and praying through them is a way of moving closer to God. As Daniel reminds us in the Apocrypha, "I do not revere man-made idols, but the living God, who created heaven and earth and has dominion over all flesh" (Daniel 14:5). Worshipping anything besides God defies the First Commandment, even though Satan constantly tempts us to do so. In our modern world, false idols take many different forms—money, fame, power—but worshipping them is like worshipping a lifeless statue because they are not divine. Nevertheless, statues remain powerful tools for repelling evil and serving as sacred conduits precisely because they connect us with God.

In the Tradition, statues of the Blessed Mother are perhaps the most common. Sometimes referred to as "sentinels of Grace," statues of Mary include various features and positions. Many depict Mary standing on a globe, representing her role as *Regina Mundi* (literally, "Queen of the World"), a title made official by Pope Pius XII. This position of dominance contrasts the widespread depiction of Mary with her hands at her sides, palms opened forward. This stance, known as the "Position of the Distribution of Graces," reminds us of Mary's role as a provider of blessings. Another frequent feature of Marian statues is the Immaculate Heart, where an exposed flaming heart encircled by a crown of golden roses marks Mary's breast. Roses and lilies remain consistent parts of Marian imagery, with the *Rosa Mundi* (or "Rose of the World") being especially effective against evil intrusions as a contrast to Satan's claim to the title of *Rex Mundi* ("King of the World"). Another flower, the lily, represents Mary's purity as the Eternal Virgin and is often incorporated into images of her. These various symbolic components serve as deterrents to the demonic, for whom Mary remains one of the primary threats among the Heavenly Host.

Perhaps the most recognizable images of the Blessed Mother are the Madonna and Child and the Pieta. The former depicts Mary holding the infant Jesus. One version of the Madonna and Child particularly repugnant to demonic entities is Our Lady of Perpetual Help. Originating from Byzantine icons, this image shows Christ's mother pointing to the infant Jesus cradled in her arms, and she is flanked by the archangels Michael and

Gabriel. This image terrifies demonic forces because it combines the sanctity of Christ and the Madonna with the ferocity of God's foremost angelic soldiers. On the other hand, statues of the Pietà represent the fulfillment of Christ's life, the Blessed Mother cradling the body of her recently crucified son Jesus evoking a powerful scene in the Tradition. Most famously captured by Michelangelo—the original stands in the vestibule of St. Peter's Basilica in Rome, widely considered to be one of the finest examples of Renaissance sculpture—the Pietà captures the sorrow of the Madonna over the torture and death of her son while also reminding us that even in the deepest moments of grief, God arms us with hope. This ultimate sacrifice, a demonstration of humility, repels Satan and his armies, who thrive on Pride, the opposite of humility.

Marian imagery is particularly widespread in Hispanic cultures, where Santa Maria holds a special place in the faith. Many of these images are directly based on the various Marian apparitions throughout history, most of which remain extremely famous, even outside the Church. One of the earliest was a vision of Mary at Guadalupe witnessed by St. Juan Diego outside of Mexico City in 1531. Our Lady of Guadalupe has a distinct appearance, robed in the regal garments of her role as Queen of Heaven. Her head is crowned with a solar nimbus (similar to a halo, referring to the "Woman clothed in the Sun" in Revelation) and stepping on a serpent, symbolizing her dominance over Satan.[83] Importantly, Our Lady of Guadalupe

---

[83] This imagery of the serpent is especially important in Mexico given its Aztec

(called by St. Pope John Paul II "the Dark Virgin of Tepeyac) is dark-skinned like the region's indigenous population, reflecting a trend increasingly common in depictions of Jesus and Mary, which reflect ethnic variations in appearance. For example, in sub-Saharan Africa, Christ and the Blessed Mother often are depicted black to reflect the ethnicity of worshippers there, while in East Asia, images of Christ reflect ethnic Asian traits. As the foremost saint of the universal Church, Mary offers protection to the faithful of every color.

Another commonly used statue of Mary is Our Lady of Lourdes. In Europe, Our Lady of Lourdes continues to draw millions of pilgrims to the French shrine every year. Copies of the original statue known as "The Virgin of the Grotto" are common throughout the Continent. The statue depicts Mary standing robed with a massive rosary around her right arm, her hands folded in prayer. This description comes from the testimony of St. Bernadette, who witnessed visions of the Blessed Mother eighteen times in 1858. During these visions, Mary revealed to St. Bernadette the location of a spring, the waters of which have been attributed to many miracles in the years since the apparition. Pilgrims to Lourdes often take with them phials of the sacred waters, liquid that is especially blessed because of its relatively recent association with Our Lady.

history. As the Mexican flag reminds us, the capital was founded on the spot where according to legend an eagle dropped a snake. The snake was a symbol of one of the major Aztec gods, Quetzalcoatl, the Plumed Serpent, so the image of Mary stepping on the snake is also a symbol of the Church converting the Aztecs.

Other popular images of Mary recall her more recent appearances. The first is Our Lady of Fatima, who appeared to three Portuguese children in 1917. Following the children's description, the Blessed Mother appears crowned and robed in white and gold, her hands folded in prayer around a rosary and her Immaculate Heart exposed. Another popular Marian statue depicts the Blessed Mother as she appeared to three children in Medjugorje, in the former Yugoslavia.

Statues of St. Joseph are extremely effective demonic deterrents as well, given Joseph's role as "Terror of Demons." As the "Guardian of the Redeemer" (a position made official by St. Pope John Paul II in his 1989 apostolic exhortation *Redemptoris custos*), Joseph symbolizes protection from evil. Traditionally, Joseph acted as the young Christ's defense against attempts by Satan to prevent the fulfillment of his mission as Savior. As a result, statues of Joseph serve as reminders to any potential demonic threats that Christ's power prevails over all evil. Although statues of Joseph alone are increasingly popular, he more often appears as part of the Holy Family, most frequently in the Nativity scene popular during the Christmas holiday. Statues of St. Joseph are also used in a custom common throughout the Catholic world: when we want to expedite the sale of our home or some other property, we bury a statue of Joseph upside down to ask for his assistance.

Other customs in the tradition involve beseeching a saint for a special purpose, usually based on their given patronage. For example, statues of St. Francis in his role of patron of animals is effective if our demonic interference involves animals in any way. This could include vexation visited through animals (such as that suffered by St. Gratus of Aosta, who was assaulted by swarms of insects) or the actual possession of animals. In cases of extreme spiritual crisis, praying through a statue of St. Jude, the patron saint of lost causes can provide the extra boost needed to achieve victory. An important point to emphasize here again is that we are praying *through* these sacred statues, not *to* them. Like the saints themselves, these statues are mediators between us and Christ, who is the sole mediator between God and us. Reverence towards the saints, and especially Mary, is therefore not equivalent to worshipping them but instead a means of demonstrating our devotion to God through his holiest representatives.

In addition to saints, statues of angels are increasingly popular. These include the well-known archangels St. Michael, St. Gabriel, and St. Raphael, all of whom stand as stalwart protectors against evil. St. Michael, in particular, offers us an abundance of protective potential. As the original vanquisher of Satan, he remains the Enemy's primary enemy among the Heavenly Host, second only to the Father and Son. As depicted in statues of the archangel, he carries both a sword and scales to mete out justice. The scales connect him with fair measure, hence his role as patron saint of grocers. In medieval portrayals of St. Michael, he is almost always stepping on Satan in the form of a dragon or serpent, the Adversary trying in vain to tip the balance of good and evil.[84] Statues of St. Michael can serve as reminders of our role as soldiers in the Church militant. Statues of St. Gabriel and St. Raphael are more difficult to distinguish, although St. Gabriel always bears a trumpet as the Herald of God and St. Raphael appears most often in his role as healer and scribe.

Beyond the popular archangels, statues of cherubs can be found in homes and gardens of the faithful. Commonly associated with the Roman god of love, Cupid, these angels appear as winged chubby children. One of the most famous examples is the cherub painted by Renaissance master Raphael (himself named after the archangel) in his *Sistine Madonna* (ca. 1515). In angelology following the systems of Thomas, Psellus, and others, the Cherubim represent the second-highest order of angels in heavenly hierarchy, below only the Seraphim. Cherubs themselves appeared on the Ark of the Covenant as described in Exodus, but starting in the Middle Ages came to represent angels in general. Cherub statues are a source of spiritual reassurance, both as messengers of the Divine and as symbols of His infinite love.

Gargoyles are another interesting type of statue. During the construction of Gothic cathedrals, gargoyles were often carved on the exterior as rainspouts. Their presence on sacred buildings might at first seem like a contradiction since they are representations of demons. In the 12th century, St. Bernard of

---

[84] Hallam, pp. 71-73

Clairvaux rejected the practice, calling them "unclean monkeys, strange savage lions and monsters." However, the gargoyle statue serves two purposes. First, gargoyles function as servants of the church building itself by funneling water away from the surface. This demeans the demons they represent to a place of servitude and inferiority. Second, gargoyle statues almost always appear on the church's exterior to demonstrate that the Light of God prevents them from entering the consecrated space. Therefore, they also serve as deterrents to any demonic entities attempting to enter that space. In the home, gargoyles in gardens and outside the walls have a similar function and remain common elements in European architecture. Placing a gargoyle statue instead, on the other hand, runs the risk of implying to demonic foes that they are welcome, emboldening them to strike us.

Other statues, such as those of pagan gods or other spirits, are widely viewed as idols and therefore break the Second Commandment. More progressive Catholics, however, embrace the idea that God works even through the benevolent spirits of other traditions and does not hold such a strict view. In many Protestant denominations, however, these idols—even those of Mary and the saints—are included in this taboo based on their literal interpretation of the Bible. In fact, the most extreme denominations do not even feature the figure of Christ on the Cross at all, just the cross itself. This parallels Islamic practice, which strictly forbids any representations of Allah or Mohammed at all, a rule that is strictly enforced. What's vital to repeat here is that statues—indeed any image or icon—used in spiritual warfare are meant to be prayed *through* as channels for positive spiritual energy, not as the objects of worship itself.

Medallions and the Scapular

Blessed medallions are a staple across traditions, but they play an especially important role in the Catholic practice. The most common blessed medallion features an image of the Blessed Mother. These images depict the Virgin Mary in her capacity as a nurturing benevolent spirit, her arms outstretched in welcome to the faithful while also serving as a bulwark against all evil influences. Images of the Madonna—Mary with the infant Jesus—are particularly powerful as they remind us, and our demonic foes, of the bond between Mary and the Son of God. Other depictions of Mary in various guises include her role as *Regina Caeli,* literally "Queen of Heaven," berobed as she is in images of Our Lady of Guadalupe and in Scriptural reference to her appearance at the End of Days: "A great and wondrous sign appeared in heaven: a woman clothed with the sun, with the moon under her feet and a crown of twelve stars on her head" (Revelation 12:1-3). On the other hand, Mary is also depicted on blessed medallions in more simple robes in her role as the Mother Immaculate. These medallions of Mary Immaculate often bear the inscription "Mary, conceived without sin, pray for us who have recourse to thee," a prayer from the Missionary

Sisters of Mary Immaculate.

Other effective medallions include those portraying St. Joseph, St. John the Beloved, or any of the apostles. Another useful icon for medallions is a personal patron saint, which could be your namesake, your confirmation saint, or the patron of your profession or hobbies. Of the apostles, one who proves useful in spiritual warfare situations which seem unmanageable is St. Jude, the patron saint of lost causes. Medallions of St. Patrick are extremely useful for protection since they invoke the Breastplate of St. Patrick, a formula used in prayers by the saint to protect the faithful against the influences of Satan and his agents.

A sacred object less familiar to non-Catholics[85] is the scapular, a band connecting two cloth rectangles with religious symbols, images of saints, or other signs of faith. The most popular scapular depicts Our Lady of Mount Carmel, after whom the Carmelite Order was named. Much like votive candles or saint statues, scapulars can generate protective positive energy through the intercessory, protecting us in a way similar to the Holy Rosary itself. Worn across the shoulder or wrapped around the wrist, scapulars can act as focuses for prayer and can stave off evil interferences.

---

[85] Scapulars are also used in the Lutheran, Anglican, and Episcopalian traditions.

Home Altars

Home altars have a long history among Christians, especially in times when access to a place of worship such as a chapel or church is restricted or not possible. In the earliest days of the Church, when Christians faced constant persecution from Roman imperial authorities, home altars were the preferred method for devout believers to practice their faith without exposing themselves to arrest, torture, or execution.

Constructing an effective home altar is relatively simple. The elements are a combination of the sacred objects we've already discussed, with the additional step of combining several such articles in a dedicated space. The first step to constructing a home altar is to find a solid crucifix, ideally a compound crucifix containing a phial of holy water, votive candles, and other sacramentals. This crucifix forms the centerpiece of the home altar. Around the crucifix, a common practice is to arrange votive candles dedicated to powerful saints, especially saints with personal relevance to the devoted and their household. This may include patron saints, nominal saints (after whom one is named, either at birth or through the Sacrament of Confirmation), or other intercessors. Votive candles are often coupled with statues of saints, especially the Virgin Mary, St. Michael, St. Gabriel, St. Joseph, and other high-ranking saints in the Canon. Holy water, chrism, and other sacramentals are also frequently set upon the altar. These spaces serve as sacred areas within the home, concentrating divine power through blessed objects and also extending this holy barrier throughout the entire home.

Daily Deeds

Practices such as home altars remind us that we can enhance our spiritual well-being in our homes. Another means of doing so is by practicing good deeds in our daily lives. This point is a crucial one in the Catholic Church. One of the primary distinctions which led to the Protestant Reformation was Martin Luther's insistence based on his interpretation of Scripture that faith alone saves, a doctrine sometimes called *solo fide*. However, while faith certainly elevates our spirits toward a state of grace, we must also practice good deeds to implement this faith. How do we accomplish this feat? One of the most effective ways is to practice the virtues and minister to society as Christ did. As St. Paul the Apostle put it, we are "Christ's ambassadors, as though God were making his appeal through us" (2 Cor. 5:20). When we perform acts of charity such as donating to the poor or helping at a homeless shelter, our deeds affirm our spiritual orientation toward Grace and away from sin. In effect, good deeds are actions that lead towards consolation and away from desolation, crucial steps to barricade our spirits against demonic influence.

Perhaps most importantly, good deeds need not be grand gestures. In fact, simple acts of kindness in our daily lives often provide us with the best spiritual nourishment because they become so habitual that we perform them without thinking. This includes actions like forgiving those who wrong us even in the slightest way, helping those around us when they are in need, and treating the people in our lives with the utmost respect and love. In his Letter to the Hebrews, St. Paul tells us "Be not forgetful to entertain strangers, for thereby some have entertained angels unawares" (13:2). Even when we may not think we are being seen, God and his holy agents see our deeds and reward us with their blessings. By doing so, we practice the paramount rule found in Christ's teachings, to treat others as we would treat ourselves. When we live a life of service, "[t]his service that you perform is not only supplying the needs of God's people but is also overflowing in many expressions of thanks to God" (2 Cor. 9:12).

Similarly, we must resist the temptation to sin, even in small ways. When we are faced with the temptation to procrastinate, we are locked in a small battle against Sloth, even if the task is small. When confronted with a desire to overeat, we struggle against Gluttony. When we resist backing down in a silly argument, we are wrestling with Pride. Sin rears its head even in the little moments, but when we reject sin, we also reject Satan. In this sense, good deeds include both what we do and what we do not do.

Lastly, we must remember that living righteously does not necessarily mean doing so for all to see. Oftentimes people perform good deeds so that others can see them and think better of them. Yet this is a form of Pride, a show of holiness that undermines itself. Instead, sometimes the most powerful acts of virtue are those we perform when no one notices: a random act of anonymous charity, helping a stranger when no one is around, forgiving our neighbors without making a production of the gesture. We must remember that even if no one witnesses our virtuous acts, we are always witnessed by the Creator. Likewise, each time we embrace a virtue and reject sin, Satan recoils from us because the grace of God shines more brightly through our illuminated spirits. Our very life of righteousness acts as a repellent against any infernal agent plotting to corrupt our homes, families, or souls.

Conclusion

We have seen that demonic entities constantly threaten us in our daily lives and in times of extreme spiritual crisis. Whether through their incarnations as spirits of Sin, as influencers who try to sway us from the righteous path, or as deceivers intent on making us believe their lies, demons walk among us. Fallen angels bound to the will of their master Satan, they thrive on our misdeeds, exploit our weaknesses, and lure us toward temptations in their quest to corrupt our souls and pollute Creation. Thankfully, through the rituals, prayers, and practices passed down to us over the last two thousand years of ecclesiastical tradition, we have the necessary tools to defeat these agents of darkness and protect ourselves, our families, and our futures.

Through our examinations of both Scripture and Tradition, we have witnessed a long history in the development of spiritual warfare, from ancient civilizations to the Middle Ages to today. This development is in many ways the evolution of our spiritual well-being as a whole and a sign that we are involved in a cosmic arms race in which the stakes couldn't be higher. When we began, we promised a set of weapons and shields against the Enemy's workings. Along the way, we have witnessed the power of the Divine manifesting in various ways. Through the Word, we have seen that bondages can be broken, curses dispelled, and demons bound. Through the Sacraments and related rituals, we have seen means of keeping Satan at bay as we attempt to avoid the temptation of sin and live virtuously as ambassadors of Christ. Through the deployment of blessed objects, saintly and angelic intercessors, and the Armor of God that is faith, we now have a fuller awareness of our allies in these battles.

We've also seen the importance of combining the practical with the theoretical, a combination too often overlooked in spiritual warfare guides. Simply knowing the prayers or going through the motions of a ritual is rarely if ever sufficient to ward off evil presences in our lives. Satan, the Prince of Lies, knows when we are lying to ourselves, and he will use any opportunity to exploit those weaknesses. Correspondingly, even if we have a complete understanding of historical encounters with the demonic, substantial knowledge of the history of spiritual warfare, prayers and sacred objects, and a thorough familiarity with Scripture in its role as the Word of God, we remain vulnerable without the practices that put this information into action. Words *and* deeds working in unison forge our sharpest weapon against Satan's machinations.

Of course, as we have seen, no spiritual warrior's training is ever done. Although we have explored many tactics and solutions, our spiritual toolkit remains incomplete because Satan never abates. Even as the Enemy continues to devise new ways to deceive us, we too need to continue our work building our arsenal. Again, vigilance is key since we must never lower our guard even after we've achieved a victory in battle. Unless we take the necessary steps to purify ourselves, our homes, and our lifestyles, no victory is secure. To achieve this goal, we must practice vigilance by maintaining focus and expanding our perceptions to discern whether darkness in our lives requires spiritual battle or some alternative solution.

The accounts of exorcists such as St. Teresa of Avila, St. John of the Cross, and Father Gabriele Amorth support the reality of these intrusions. The various narratives from the lives of the saints—from St. Michael the Archangel to St. Paul the Apostle to St. Catherine of Siena—give us advanced tools for any spiritual warfare situation. We have armed ourselves with both spiritual weapons and shields. We have come to an understanding that spiritual warfare can involve both terrifying struggles with the satanic and small intrusions in our lives that can lead to suffering for ourselves and others. We have seen demonic entities threaten our families, relationships, and careers. Most importantly, we have learned the techniques for identifying demonic activity so we can dispel it with the proper course of action. We now know how to destroy what needs to be destroyed and how to protect what needs to be protected.

Hopefully, any reader who came to this book with doubts about the role of demons in our lives has come to understand the threats they pose and the tactics they use to deceive us. Whether through vexations, oppressions, possessions, infestations, or any other demonic influence, demons constantly seek to undermine our faith and sow chaos in our lives. Rather than simply list prayers, we have seen the context of their origins, discussed instances when they are most effective, and investigated cases of these prayers in action. We have determined which soldiers in the Heavenly Host can best come to our aid in our hour of need and reaffirmed our pledge to serve alongside them as soldiers of Light. We have also discussed at length the importance of distinguishing spiritual crises from psychological disturbances, especially given the similarities between the two. Even the most adamant doubter can see in the accounts of saints, exorcists, and laypeople that science and reason alone cannot replace these invaluable instructions in spiritual warfare.

As promised at the outset, this book is intended to open readers' hearts to the possibilities of God's grace as weapons against evil in our lives. The ultimate source of these weapons is God's love, but we've also come to understand that love is reflected in our deeds and attitudes towards others. When we live like Christ, we become like Him and repel Satan's operatives' advances. When we hold steadfast in our faith, we can know nothing but victory. Through a combination of liturgical prayers, sacred objects, and living virtuously, we discovered that the works of Satan, once dispelled, can be exiled from our lives forever. Victory can not only be achieved—it can also be preserved.

As we part ways, remember first and foremost that everyone has the potential to become a soldier of Light. Regardless of age, ethnicity, or political affiliation, we will all encounter demonic workings at some point in our lives, whether we are aware of it. In this book, we have focused on the traditions handed down through the Church and related Catholic mystical practice, but no matter one's religion, the Divine is always willing to offer aid when agents of evil attempt to attack us. So long as we are willing to keep our hearts open, our eyes sharp, and our tongues prepared, Satan will always find in us prey capable of resisting him. Like the Blessed Virgin Mary or the Lord Himself, we can crush the head of the serpent. Equipped now with the Sword of Christ, the Armor of God, and the Spears of the Heavenly Host of saints and angels, we can march forward into spiritual battle, assured that we are not alone on the path to eternal victory over the Enemy.

Last message and small request from the author:

I wish you nothing but protection from God and your faith in knowing He's there to always protect you and to always fight your battles with you. You are not alone on your journey toward spiritual warfare.

If you've enjoyed this book or found that it has been exactly what you've needed, please consider leaving the book a review.

All feedback is extremely important to me as an independent author. It helps me deliver exactly what you want, and it also helps other readers make a decision when deciding on the best books to purchase. I would greatly appreciate it if you could take 60 seconds to leave the book a quick review. You can also reach out via email to leave any feedback.

Email: UltimateGuidance1111@gmail.com

God Bless,

Caleb E Benedict

References

A., Boron, R. D., & Wheatley, H. B. (2012). *Merlin, or The Early History of King Arthur: A Prose Romance.* Lexicos Publishing.

Amorth, G. (1999). *An Exorcist Tells His Story.* Ignatius Press.

Amorth, G., & Fasi, C. J. (2016). *Exorcist Explains the Demonic.* Sophia Institute Press.

Aquino, M. A., LaVey, S. Z., LaVey, D., & S. (2018). *The Satanic Bible: 50th Anniversary ReVision* (Anniversary, Revised ed.). CreateSpace Independent Publishing Platform.

Berg, M. (2017). *Fear Is Not An Option* (First ed.). Kabbalah Centre Publishing.

Blai, A. C. (2017). *Hauntings, Possessions, and Exorcisms.* Emmaus Road Publishing.

Blank, S. H. (1950). The Curse, The Blasphemy, The Spell, and the Oath. *Hebrew Union College Annual* 23(1).

Burn, A. E. (1909). *The Nicene creed.* London: Rivingtons

Burke, D. (2020). *Spiritual Warfare and The Discernment of Spirits.* Sophia

Institute Press.

Buterin, T., Muzur, A. & Glažar, B. (2021). "Saints and "Possession": A Case Review Bordering Ethnopsychiatry and Cultural Diversity. *J Relig Health* 60, 1116–1124.

Campbell, J. (2008). *The Hero with a Thousand Faces (The Collected Works of Joseph Campbell)* (Third ed.). New World Library.

Christe, I. (2004). *Sound of the Beast: The Complete Headbanging History of Heavy Metal* (First ed.). It Books.

Connolly, S. (2011). *Curses, Hexes & Crossing: A Magician's Guide to Execration Magick*. CreateSpace Independent Publishing Platform.

Crisogono del Jesus Sacramentado (1974). Vida y Obras de San Juan de la Crus. Biblioteca de Autores Cristianos.

Driscoll, J.F. (1911). St. Raphael. In *The Catholic Encyclopedia*. Robert Appleton Company.

Eckhardt, J. (2014). *Deliverance and Spiritual Warfare Manual: A Comprehensive Guide to Living Free*. Charisma House.

Evola, J. (2021). *Metaphysics of War*. Arktos Media Ltd.

Foucault, M. (2020). *The Foucault Reader: Michel Foucault (Penguin Modern Classics)* (1st ed.). Penguin Classics.

Frazer, J. G. (2022). *The Golden Bough: A Study of Magic and Religion*. Penguin.

Giglio, L. (2022). *Don't Give the Enemy a Seat at Your Table: It's Time to Win the Battle of Your Mind*. Harper Christian Resources.

Greenbaum, D. G. (2015). *The Daimon in Hellenistic Astrology*. Brill.

Gunter, S. (1994). *PRAYER PORTIONS SAMPLER FOR THE FAMILY*. Father's Business Press.

Hallam, E. (1994). *Saints: Who They Are and How They Help You* (Eddison Sadd ed). Simon & Schuster.

Jeremiah, D. (2016). *The Spiritual Warfare Answer Book (Answer Book Series)*. Thomas Nelson.

John of the Cross (1979). *The Collected Works of St. John of the Cross*. Trans. by Kieren Kavanaugh, OCD and Otilio Rodriguez, OCD. Institute of Carmelite Studies.

Ibanez, Pedro, OP. *The Complete Works of St. Teresa of Jesus*. Trans. by E. Allison Peers. New York: Sheed and Ward, 1946.

Kiperwasser, R. (2021). Solomon and Ashmedai Redux: Redaction Criticism of bGitin68b. *Jewish Quarterly Review* 111(1), 21-54.

Kitz, A.M. (2014). "The Grammar of Curses." *Cursed Are You!* Penn State Press.

Lancaster, D. B. (2016). *Powerful Prayers in the War Room: Learning to Pray like a Powerful Prayer Warrior (Spiritual Battle Plan for Prayer)*. CreateSpace Independent Publishing Platform.

LeClaire, J. (2021). *Decoding the Mysteries of Heaven's War Room: 21 Heavenly Strategies for Powerful Prayer and Triumphant Warfare*. Destiny Image Publishers.

Leclercq, H. (1910). Holy Water. In *The Catholic Encyclopedia*. New York: Robert Appleton Company.

Lepee, M. (1972). "St. Teresa of Jesus and the Devil." In Satan. Ed. by Bruno de Jesus-Marie, OCD. Sheed and Ward.

Lewis, C. S. (2021). *The Screwtape Letters*. Sanage Publishing House.

Lucien-Marie de Saint Joseph (1972). "The Devil in the Writings of St. John of the Cross." In *Satan*. Ed. by Bruno de Jesus-Marie, OCD. Sheed and Ward.

Markos, L. (2021). *From Plato to Christ: How Platonic Thought Shaped the*

Christian Faith. IVP Academic.

Madueke, P. M. (2021). *Evil Presence: Total Destruction of Demonic Possession & Oppression in Homes, Body Organs, Offices & Properties. Enough Is Enough (Satanic and Demonic . . . Breaking Demonic Curses, Cast Out Demons).* Independently published.

Marlowe, C. (2020). *The Tragical History of Doctor Faustus* (1st ed.). Delhi Open Books.

Martinez, S., & Strieber, W. (2019). *Field Guide to the Spirit World: The Science of Angel Power, Discarnate Entities, and Demonic Possession.* Bear & Company.

McAlister, E. (2015). "Prayer in Wider Perspective: Spiritual Warfare and Aggressive Prayers," Reverberations: New Directions in the Study of Prayer.

Milton, J., & Teskey, G. (2020). *Paradise Lost (Norton Critical Editions)* (Second ed.). W. W. Norton & Company.

Moreno, A. (2022). *Demons According to St. Teresa and St. John of the Cross.* Catholic Culture. https://www.catholicculture.org/culture/library/view.cfm?recnum=8280

Myles, F. (2021). *Dangerous Prayers from the Courts of Heaven that Destroy Evil Altars: Establishing the Legal Framework for Closing Demonic Entryways and Breaking Generational Chains of Darkness.* Destiny Image Publishers.

Nietzsche, F. (2013). *On the genealogy of morality* (R. C. Holub, Ed.; M. A. Scarpitti, Trans.).

Nietzsche, F. W., Hollingdale, R. J., & Tanner, M. (1990). *Beyond good and evil: Prelude to a philosophy of the future.* London, England: Penguin Books.

O'Leary, D. L. & Society for Promoting Christian Knowledge (1906). *The Apostolic Constitutions and Cognate Documents with Special Reference to*

References

Their Liturgica Elements. Society for Promoting Christian Knowledge.

Osterreich, T. K. (2012). *The Nature of the State of Demonic Possession - A Classic Article on the History and Subjective State of Demonic Possession.* Owens Press.

Paul VI (2017, April 7). *Confronting The Devil's Power.* Papal Encyclicals. https://www.papalencyclicals.net/paul06/p6devil.htm

Payne, K. (2021). *Spiritual Warfare: Christians, Demonization and Deliverance* (Second edition). Republic Book Publishers.

Platt, M. M. (2012). *Storming the Gates of Bedlam; How Dr. Nathan Kline Transformed the Treatment of Mental Illness.* DePew Publishing.

Rasmussen, J. (2019). *How Reason Can Lead to God: A Philosopher's Bridge to Faith.* IVP Academic.

Ripperger, C. (2016). *Deliverance Prayers: For Use by the Laity* (1st ed.). CreateSpace Independent Publishing Platform.

Rodkinson, L. M. (2018). *The Babylonian Talmud: Original Text, Edited, Corrected, Formulated, and Translated Into English; Section Jurisprudence (Damages), Tract Sanhedrin; Volumes VII. And VII. (XV. And XVI.).* Forgotten Books.

Sales, D. S. F., D.Min., O. R., & de Sales, M. O. S. F. (2019). *Introduction to the Devout Life.*

Opened Heart LLC.

Sargant, W. W. (1974). *The mind possessed;: A physiology of possession, mysticism, and faith healing.* Lippincott.

Savchuk, V. (2020). *Fight Back: Moving from Deliverance to Dominion (Spiritual Warfare).* Independently published.

Shakespeare, W., Bate, J., & Rasmussen, E. (2022). *William Shakespeare Complete Works Second Edition (Modern Library)* (2nd ed.). Modern

Library.

Sherrer, Q., & Garlock, R. (2017). *A Woman's Guide to Spiritual Warfare: How to Protect Your Home, Family and Friends from Spiritual Darkness* (Revised and Updated ed.). Chosen Books.

Silf, M. (2003). *Close to the Heart: A Guide to Personal Prayer* (First ed.). Loyola Press. ---. (2012). *Simple Faith: Moving Beyond Religion as You Know It to Grow in Your Relationship with God* (First ed.). Loyola Press. Stagnaro, A. (2016). "Blessed Bartolo Longo, the Ex-Satanist Who Was Freed Through the Rosary." *National Catholic Register*, Dec. 12, 2016.

Stanzione, A. W. M. (2020). *The Devil is Afraid of Me: The Life and Work of the World's Most Popular Exorcist*. Sophia Institute Press.

Strachan, F. (1972). *Casting Out the Devils* (First Edition). Samuel Weiser Inc.

Teresa of Jesus (1961). *Autobiography of St. Teresa of Avila*. Trans. by E. Allison Peers. Garden City, Image Books. ---. (1946). *Complete Works of Teresa of Jesus*. Trans. by E. Allison Peers. New York: Sheed and Ward.

Thigpen, P. (2014). *Manual for Spiritual Warfare* (Lea ed.). TAN Books. ---. (2015). *Saints Who Battled Satan: Seventeen Holy Warriors Who Can Teach You How to Fight the Good Fight and Vanquish Your Ancient Enemy*. TAN Books.

Thurman, H. (1963). *Disciplines of the Spirit (Howard Thurman Book)* (Reprint ed.). Friends United Press.

Tolstoy, N. (1985). *The Quest for Merlin* (1st American ed). Little, Brown.

Tonquedec Joseph de. SJ. (1972). "Some Aspects of Satan's Activity in this World." In *Satan*. Ed. by Bruno de Jesus-Marie, OCD. New York: Sheed and Ward..

von Goethe, J. W., Hamlin, C., & Arndt, W. W. (1998). *Faust: A*

Tragedy (Norton Critical Editions) (Second ed.). W. W. Norton & Company.

von Nettesheim, A. H. C., & Compagni, P. V. (1992). *De Occulta Philosophia Libri Tres, Vol. 48 (Studies in the History of Christian Traditions)*. Brill Academic Pub.

Weigel, G. (2017). *Lessons in Hope: My Unexpected Life with St. John Paul II* (New ed.). Basic Books.

Weller, P. T. (2022). *Roman Ritual 3 Volume Set*. Preserving Christian Publications.

White, V. (1965). *God and the Unconscious*. Meridian Books.

Woods, Richard OP. (1972). "Satanism Today." In *Soundings in Satanism*. New York: Sheed and Ward.

###

Made in United States
Orlando, FL
02 June 2025

61787444R00171